Special Education Eligibility

This book is dedicated to my wife, Jackie,
and my two children, Jacqueline and Scott,
who provide me with the love and purpose for
undertaking projects that I hope will enhance the lives of
others. My life has been blessed by their loving presence.
I also dedicate this book to my parents, who provided me with
the secure and loving foundation from which to grow; my sister,
Carol, who makes me smile and laugh; and my brother-in-law, George,
who has always been a positive guiding light in my professional journey.

—R. P.

This book is dedicated to my wife, Anita,
and two children, Collin and Brittany, who give me the
greatest life imaginable. The long hours and many years
it took to finish this book would never have been possible
without the support of my loving wife. Her constant encouragement,
understanding, and love provide me with the strength I need to
accomplish my goals. I thank her with all my heart. I also dedicate
this book to my parents, who have given me support and guidance
throughout my life. Their words of encouragement and guidance
have made my professional journey a rewarding and successful experience.

—G. G.

A STEP-BY-STEP GUIDE FOR EDUCATORS

Special Education Eligibility

ROGER PIERANGELO ~ GEORGE GIULIANI

CORWIN PRESS
A SAGE Publications Company
Thousand Oaks, CA 91320

For information:

Corwin Press
A Sage Publications Company
2455 Teller Road
Thousand Oaks, California 91320
www.corwinpress.com

Sage Publications Ltd.
1 Oliver's Yard
55 City Road
London, EC1Y 1SP
United Kingdom

Sage Publications India Pvt. Ltd.
B 1/I 1 Mohan Cooperative
   Industrial Area
Mathura Road, New Delhi 110 044
India

Sage Publications Asia-Pacific Pte. Ltd.
33 Pekin Street #02-01
Far East Square
Singapore 048763

Printed in the United States of America

Library of Congress Cataloging-in-Publication Data

Pierangelo, Roger.
Special education eligibility : a step-by-step guide for educators / Roger Pierangelo, George Giuliani.
      p. cm.
Includes bibliographical references and index.
ISBN 978-1-4129-5423-5 (cloth)
ISBN 978-1-4129-1785-8 (pbk.)
    1. Special education—United States. I. Giuliani, George A., 1938- II. Title.

LC3981.P539 2007
371.90973—dc22   2006102667

This book is printed on acid-free paper.

07 08 09 10 11   10 9 8 7 6 5 4 3 2 1

Acquisitions Editor:	Allyson P. Sharp
Editorial Assistant:	Nadia Kashper
Production Editor:	Laureen A. Shea
Typesetter:	C&M Digitals (P) Ltd.
Proofreader:	Victoria Reed-Castro
Cover Designer:	Michael Dubowe

Contents

Preface

S pecial Education Eligibility: A Step-by-Step Guide for Educators focuses on understanding the eligibility criteria and process for students with suspected disabilities. The term *special education eligibility* refers to a series of criteria that are used to determine whether a student meets the requirements under the federal law (Individuals with Disabilities Education Improvement Act of 2004) as a "student with a disability."

There are many reasons why a teacher would need to know about the eligibility requirements for students with special needs. The most important reasons include the following:

- To understand how the classifications of the students in your classroom were derived
- To understand how to make an appropriate **diagnosis** when you attend an **individualized education program (IEP)** or Committee on Special Education meeting
- To be able to render a professional opinion about whether a student's classification is no longer an appropriate one or needs to be changed as a result of developing and new factors
- To be able to explain to parents or guardians how eligibility may be determined should the parent or guardian be considering an assessment for special education services
- To have a consistent format for making eligibility determinations when working with the **student study team** and making a referral for a student with a suspected disability
- To use as a reference guide when you are unclear about how various classifications are determined under the law

Special Education Eligibility: A Step-by-Step Guide for Educators takes you through a step-by-step process, so that you will have a basic overview of how all the various classifications under the federal law for special education are determined.

Acknowledgments

In the course of writing this book, we have encountered many professional and outstanding sites. Those resources have contributed and continue to contribute enormous information, support, guidance, and education to parents, students, and professionals in the area of special education. Although we have accessed many worthwhile sites, we especially thank and acknowledge the National Dissemination Center for Children with Disabilities, the Alaska State Department of Education, and the National Institutes of Health.

    Dr. Roger Pierangelo and Dr. George Giuliani extend sincere thanks to Allyson Sharp and Laureen Shea at Corwin Press. Their constant encouragement and professionalism made this project a very worthwhile and rewarding experience.

Roger Pierangelo: I extend thanks to the following: the faculty, administration, and staff of the Department of Graduate Special Education and Literacy at Long Island University; Ollie Simmons, for her friendship, loyalty, and great personality; the students and parents of the Herricks Public Schools I have worked with and known over the past thirty-five years; the late Bill Smyth, a truly gifted and "extraordinary ordinary" man; and Helen Firestone, for her influence on my career and her tireless support of me.

George Giuliani: I extend sincere thanks to all of my colleagues at Hofstra University in the School of Education and Allied Human Services. I am especially grateful to those who have made my transition to Hofstra University such a smooth one, including Maureen Murphy (dean), Daniel Sciarra (chairperson), Frank Bowe, Diane Schwartz (graduate program director of early childhood special education), Darra Pace, Gloria Wilson, Alan Wenderoff, Laurie Johnson, Joan Bloomgarden, Jamie Mitus, Estelle Gellman, Joseph Lechowicz, Holly Seirup, Adele Piombino, Marjorie Butler, Eve Byrne, and Linda Cappa. I also thank my brother and sister, Roger and Claudia; mother-in-law Ursula Jenkeleit; sisters-in-law Karen and Cindy; and brothers-in-law Robert and Bob. They have provided me with encouragement and reinforcement in all of my personal and professional endeavors.

Corwin Press gratefully acknowledges the contributions of the following reviewers:

Heather M. Baltodano
Assistant Professor
Eastern Kentucky University
Richmond, KY

Joyce Williams Bergin
Professor and Graduate Coordinator
Armstrong Atlantic State University
Savannah, GA

Iris Goldberg
Director Early Childhood/Childhood Programs
Westchester Graduate Campus of Long Island University
Purchase, NY

Jo-Anne Goldberg
Director of Special Education
Mainland Regional High School
Linwood, NJ

Lori Ann Schwab
Exceptional Needs Specialist, NBCT
Golden Terrace Elementary-Intermediate School
Naples, FL

Kimberly Thomas
Exceptional Children's Teacher
Union County Public Schools
Monroe, NC

Pamela Wall
Teacher
Mauldin Elementary School
Simpsonville, NC

About the Authors

Roger Pierangelo, PhD, is an associate professor in the Department of Special Education and Literacy at Long Island University. He has been an administrator of special education programs, served for eighteen years as a permanent member of Committees on Special Education, has over thirty years of experience in the public school system as a general education classroom teacher and school psychologist, and serves as a consultant to numerous private and public schools, PTA, and SEPTA groups. Dr. Pierangelo has also been an evaluator for the New York State Office of Vocational and Rehabilitative Services and a director of a private clinic. He is a New York State–licensed clinical psychologist, a certified school psychologist, and a Board Certified Diplomate Fellow in Student and Adolescent Psychology and Forensic Psychology. Dr. Pierangelo is the executive director of the National Association of Special Education Teachers (NASET) and an executive director of the American Academy of Special Education Professionals (AASEP). He also holds the office of vice president of the National Association of Parents with Children in Special Education (NAPCSE).

Dr. Pierangelo earned his BS from St. John's University, MS from Queens College, Professional Diploma from Queens College, PhD from Yeshiva University, and Diplomate Fellow in Student and Adolescent Psychology and Forensic Psychology from the International College of Professional Psychology. Dr. Pierangelo is a member of the American Psychological Association, New York State Psychological Association, Nassau County Psychological Association, New York State Union of Teachers, and Phi Delta Kappa.

Dr. Pierangelo is the author of multiple books by Corwin Press, including *The Big Book of Special Education Resources* and *The Step-by-Step Series for Special Educators.*

George Giuliani, JD, PsyD, is a full-time tenured associate professor and the director of Special Education at Hofstra University's School of Education and Allied Human Services in the Department of Counseling, Research, Special Education, and Rehabilitation. Dr. Giuliani earned his BA from the College of the Holy Cross, MS from St. John's University, JD from City University Law School, and PsyD from Rutgers University, the Graduate School of Applied and Professional Psychology. He earned Board Certification as a Diplomate Fellow in Student and Adolescent Psychology and Forensic Psychology from the International College of Professional Psychology. Dr. Giuliani is also a New York State–licensed psychologist and certified school psychologist and has an extensive private practice focusing on students with special needs. He is a member of the American Psychological Association, New York State Psychological Association, National Association of School Psychologists, Suffolk County Psychological Association, Psi Chi, American Association of University Professors, and the Council for Exceptional Students.

Dr. Giuliani is the president of the National Association of Parents with Children in Special Education (NAPCSE), executive director of the National Association of Special Education Teachers (NASET), and executive director of the American Academy of Special Education Professionals (AASEP). He is a consultant for school districts and early childhood agencies and has provided numerous workshops for parents and guardians and teachers on a variety of special education and psychological topics. Dr. Giuliani is the coauthor of numerous books by Corwin Press, including *The Big Book of Special Education Resources* and *The Step-by-Step Series for Special Educators.*

1

Overview of Special Education and Eligibility Procedures

Brief History of the Individuals with Disabilities Education Act

The Individuals with Disabilities Education Act (IDEA) is a federal law that supports special education and **related service** programming for students and youth with disabilities. It was formerly known as the Education for the Handicapped Act (EHA). IDEA has its roots in Public Law (PL) 94-142 (the Education of All Handicapped Students Act), which was originally enacted in 1975 to establish grants to states for the education of students with disabilities. This law has been amended several times. Under Part B of the law, all eligible school-aged students and youth with disabilities are entitled to receive a **free appropriate public education (FAPE).**

In 1986, the EHA was amended by PL 99-457 to provide special funding incentives for states that would make FAPE available for all eligible preschool-aged students, ages 3 through 5, with disabilities. Provisions were also included to help states develop early **intervention** programs for infants and toddlers with disabilities; this part of the legislation became known as the Part H Program. In 1997, when the amendments to IDEA were authorized, this section of the law that applied to infants and toddlers was changed to Part C.

The EHA was amended again in 1990 by PL 101-476, which, among other things, changed the name of the legislation to the Individuals with Disabilities Education Act, or IDEA. IDEA was first amended in 1992 by PL 102-119. The newest amendments to this law are the Individuals with Disabilities Education Act Amendments of 1997 (PL 105-17). These amendments restructured IDEA into four parts: Part A addresses General Provisions; Part B covers the Assistance for Education of All Students with Disabilities; Part C covers Infants and Toddlers with Disabilities; and Part D addresses National Activities to Improve the Education of Students with Disabilities.

On December 3, 2004, the Individuals with Disabilities Education Improvement Act of 2004 was enacted into law as PL 108-446. The statute, as passed by Congress and signed by President George W. Bush, reauthorized and made significant changes to IDEA.

IDEA, as amended by the Individuals with Disabilities Education Improvement Act of 2004, seeks to help students with disabilities achieve high educational standards by promoting accountability for results, enhancing parent or guardian involvement, using proven practices and materials, and providing more flexibility and reducing paperwork burdens for teachers, states, and local school districts.

The new law provides for improvements in the current regulations, whereby every student with a disability is ensured an FAPE that (1) is of high quality and (2) will help each such student achieve the high standards reflected in the Elementary and Secondary Education Act of 1965, as amended by the No Child Left Behind Act of 2001 (NCLB) and its implementing regulations.

Purposes of IDEA

The major purposes of IDEA are as follows:

- To ensure that all students with disabilities have access to FAPE that emphasizes special education and related services designed to meet their unique needs and to prepare them for employment and independent living
- To ensure that the rights of students and youth with disabilities and their parents or guardians are protected

- To assist states, localities, educational service agencies, and federal agencies to provide for the education of all students with disabilities
- To assess and ensure the effectiveness of efforts to educate students with disabilities

Special Education

Special education is instruction that is specially designed, at no cost to parents or guardians, to meet a student's unique needs. Specially designed instruction means adapting the content, methodology, or delivery of instruction in order to fulfill the following objectives:

- To address the unique needs of the student that result from his or her disability
- To ensure the student's access to the general curriculum so that he or she can meet the educational standards that apply to all students within the jurisdiction of the public agency

Special education can include instruction conducted in the classroom, in the home, in hospitals and institutions, and in other settings. It can also include instruction in physical education. Under state standards, speech-language pathology services or any other related service can be considered special education rather than a related service providing the instruction is specially designed, at no cost to the parents or guardians, to meet the unique needs of a student with a disability. Travel training and vocational education that meet these standards can also be considered special education.

Student With a Disability

As delineated in IDEA 2004, a student with a disability is one who has been *evaluated as having mental retardation, a hearing impairment (including deafness), a speech or language impairment, a visual impairment (including blindness), a serious emotional disturbance, an orthopedic impairment, autism, traumatic brain injury, an other [sic] health impairment, a specific **learning disability,** deaf-blindness, or multiple disabilities, and who, by reason thereof, needs special education and related services.*

For students ages 3 through 9, a "student with a disability" may include a student who is experiencing *developmental delays*. Such a definition must originate from the state and be measured by appropriate diagnostic instruments and procedures, in one or more of the following areas: physical development, cognitive development, communication development, social or emotional development, adaptive development, *and* who, for that reason, needs special education and related services.

From birth through age 2, students may be eligible for services through the Infants and Toddlers with Disabilities Program (Part C) of IDEA.

Disabilities Covered Under IDEA

Under IDEA, a student with a disability may have one or more of the following disabling conditions (Authority: 20 U.S.C. 1401(3); 1401(30)):

- Autism
- Deaf-blindness
- Deafness
- Developmental delay
- Emotional disturbance
- Hearing impairment
- Mental retardation
- Multiple disabilities
- Orthopedic impairment
- Other health impairment
- Specific learning disability
- Speech or language impairment
- Traumatic brain injury
- Visual impairment

Evaluation for Special Education

When a student is referred for a suspected disability, an individual evaluation of the student takes place, providing the parent or guardian has given consent to do the evaluation (written permission). This evaluation involves formal tests, informal assessment measures, observations, interviews, and other assessment measures deemed necessary. Through this evaluation, the school can determine whether the student has a disability and whether that student will need special services. The evaluation also attempts to determine whether certain factors unrelated to the disability may be affecting the student in school. The results of the evaluation are then used as a guide to develop the student's educational program and to determine whether adjustments to the student's educational program will be necessary.

Components of a Comprehensive Evaluation

An evaluation for a suspected disability should constitute a comprehensive assessment of the student's abilities. Professionals involved in the evaluation process can use numerous tests to evaluate the student's suspected disability; it is important that these tests be administered on an individual basis. Most of these tests are either **norm-referenced** or **criterion-referenced.** *Norm-referenced tests* are those tests that are standardized on groups of individuals and that measure a student's performance relative to the performance of a group with similar characteristics. District, state, or national offices usually administer norm-referenced tests.

Criterion-referenced tests measure a student's **achievement** or development relative to a specific standard. Such tests are especially useful for planning instruction or for measuring curriculum content mastery because they can correspond closely to curriculum content and classroom instruction. The classroom teacher generally selects or develops, as well as administers, criterion-referenced tests.

Specifically, these assessment measures may include but are not limited to

- Individual psychological evaluation (when determined necessary by the multidisciplinary team), including general intelligence, instructional needs, learning strengths and weaknesses, and social emotional dynamics. A licensed school psychologist completes this measure.
- Social history taken by either a social worker or a school psychologist
- Physical examination, including specific assessments that relate to vision, hearing, and general health, conducted by either the school physician or the student's own doctor
- Observation of the student in his or her current educational setting, usually by another teacher, most likely a special education teacher

- Appropriate educational evaluation specifically pinpointing the areas of **deficit** or suspected disability, including but not limited to educational achievement, academic needs, learning strengths and weaknesses, vocational assessments
- Vocational assessments by professional vocational or rehabilitation counselors, work study evaluators, or guidance counselors if the student is of age (14 years and older)
- **Bilingual** assessment for students with limited English proficiency, conducted in the student's **native language**

The Eligibility Committee/IEP Committee

The Eligibility Committee, which is also referred to as the IEP Committee, is responsible for developing a recommendation statement that addresses the student's individual educational needs. By law, parents and guardians are invited to Eligibility Committee/IEP Committee meetings and are encouraged to participate in developing the recommendation together with the committee members. Based on the evaluations completed by the designees and the district evaluators, the Eligibility Committee decides whether the student meets the criteria for a disability and is entitled to special education services.

If the student does not require special education, the Eligibility Committee/IEP Committee forwards copies of the recommendation to the parents or guardians, the building administrator, and the board of education. The recommendation states the Eligibility Committee's/IEP Committee's findings and specifies that educational services other than special education, such as speech and language improvement services, be considered. The Eligibility Committee/IEP Committee should determine what, if any, educationally related support services should be provided to the student.

If the student does require special education, an IEP will be developed for the student. This IEP will include the specific type of disability; describe the student's strengths and areas of need; list goals that the student should reach in a year's time; include short-term instructional objectives that represent a series of specific skills to be mastered; set out **annual goals** for the student; and identify the types of programs and services, including general education, that the student will receive. This information is included on the student's IEP; one copy of the recommendation is sent to the board of education for approval and another to the parent or guardian for his or her records.

Responsibilities of the Eligibility Committee/IEP Committee

The district's Eligibility Committee

- Reviews and evaluates all relevant information that may appear on each student with a disability
- Determines the least restrictive educational setting for any student classified as having a disability
- Follows appropriate procedures and takes appropriate action on any student referred as having a suspected disability
- Determines the suitable classification for a student with a suspected disability
- Reviews, at least annually, the status of each student with a disability residing within the district
- Evaluates the adequacy of programs, services, and facilities for the students with disabilities in the district
- Maintains ongoing communication in writing to the parents or guardians in regard to planning, modifying, changing, reviewing, placing, or evaluating the program, classification, or educational plan for a student with disabilities
- Advises the board of education as to the status and recommendations for all students with disabilities in the district

Members of the Eligibility Committee/IEP Committee

Membership of the Eligibility Committee/IEP Committee includes school division personnel representing the disciplines that provide assessments (e.g., school psychologist, speech language clinician, school nurse), the special education administrator or designee (someone standing in for the special education administrator assigned by the district), the student's classroom teacher, and the parents or guardians. At least one representative on the committee must have either assessed or observed the student. Other members can include professionals who have worked with the student outside of the classroom, attorneys, and any other individual who may be appropriate. Finally, the student can attend the meeting, which is often the case when the student is over the age of 14 years old.

Procedures for Determining Eligibility

The members of the Eligibility Committee/IEP Committee who make the decision regarding the student's eligibility are expected to work until they reach consensus. The school district has to obtain parent or guardian consent for the initial eligibility determination. Thereafter, parent or guardian consent needs to be secured for any change in the student's special education classification.

The Eligibility Committee issues a written summary that sets forth its basis for its determination as to the student's eligibility for special education and related services. Each committee member present at the meeting signs the summary. The written summary is henceforth maintained in the student's scholastic record, and the district gives the parent or guardian a copy of all of the documentation used in determining the student's classification and educational placement.

No changes can be made to a student's classification and placement for special education and related services without parent or guardian consent.

2

Autism

Definition Under IDEA

> *A developmental disability significantly affecting verbal and nonverbal communication and social interaction, usually evident before age 3 that adversely affects a student's educational performance. Other characteristics often associated with autism are engagement in repetitive activities and stereotyped movements, resistance to environmental change or change in daily routines, and unusual responses to sensory experiences. The term does not apply if a student's educational performance is adversely affected because the student has an emotional disturbance.* (34 C.F.R. 300.7(a)(c)(1)(i))

Overview

Autism is a *spectrum disorder*. That is, the symptoms and characteristics of autism can present themselves in a wide variety of combinations, from mild to severe. Although autism is defined by a certain set of behaviors, students and adults with autism spectrum disorder (ASD) can exhibit *any combination* of the behaviors in *any degree of severity*. Two students, both with the same diagnosis, can act very differently from one another and have varying skills.

Originally described in 1943 by Leo Kanner, autism is a behavioral syndrome, which means that its definition is based on a person's patterns of behaviors. Individuals with autism and ASD vary widely in ability and personality. Some individuals with these syndromes can exhibit severe mental retardation or be extremely gifted intellectually and academically. Whereas many such individuals prefer isolation and tend to withdraw from social contact, others show high levels of affection and enjoyment in social situations. Some people with autism appear lethargic and slow to respond, with more focus on objects than on people. Others are very active and seem to interact constantly with preferred aspects of their environment.

Parents or guardians are usually the first to notice unusual behaviors in their child. In some cases, the baby seemed "different" from birth, unresponsive to people or focusing intently on one item for long periods of time. The first signs of autism can also appear in children who seem to have been developing normally. When an engaging, babbling toddler suddenly becomes silent, withdrawn, self-abusive, or indifferent to social overtures, something is wrong. Research has shown that parents or guardians are usually correct in their detection of developmental problems, although they may not realize the specific nature or degree of the problem.

All students with ASD demonstrate deficits in (1) social interaction, (2) verbal and nonverbal communication, and (3) repetitive behaviors or interests. In addition, they will often have unusual responses to sensory experiences, such as certain sounds or the way objects look. Each of these symptoms runs the gamut from mild to severe and will present in each individual student differently. For instance, a student may have little trouble learning to read but exhibit extremely poor social interaction. Each student will display communication, social, and behavioral patterns that are individual but fit into the overall diagnosis of ASD.

Students with ASD do not follow the typical patterns of student development. In some students, hints of future problems may be apparent to the parent or guardian from birth. In most cases, the problems in communication and social skills become more noticeable as the student lags further behind other students the same age. In other cases, children may start off well enough, but often, between 12 and 36 months of age, the parent or guardian will recognize differences in the way they react to people and other unusual behaviors. Some parents or guardians report that the change is sudden and that the child starts to reject people, act strangely, and lose language and social skills that had previously been acquired. In other cases, a plateau, or leveling, of progress takes place so that the difference between children with autism and other children the same age becomes more noticeable.

Prevalence

According to the *Twenty-Sixth Annual Report* of the U.S. Department of Education (2004), 140,473 students between the ages of 6 and 21 were identified as having autism. This represents approximately 2.3 percent of all students having a classification in special education and approximately 0.12 percent of all school-age students.

Determining the Presence of Autism: Step by Step

Step I: Become Familiar With the Characteristics of Students With Autism

The following are the most common signs and symptoms of a student with autism:

- The student exhibits impairments in communication.
- The student exhibits impairments in social interaction.
- The student exhibits patterns of behavior, interests, and/or activities that are restricted, repetitive, or stereotypic.
- The student exhibits unusual responses to sensory information.

The Student Who Shows a Number of Impairments in Communication

- Has an abnormal tone and rhythm in speech
- Begins to develop babbling and then stops
- Starts to develop language and then suddenly stops
- Cries about things that are not related to needs
- Shows delay in, or lack of, development of spoken language
- Has difficulty understanding gestures and using compensatory nonverbal language
- Has difficulty with comprehension
- Finds it difficult to stick to the topic
- Fails to imitate sounds, gestures, or expressions
- Is nonresponsive to his or her name
- Does not volunteer information or initiate speech
- Is not able to follow simple directions, or to follow directions out of the usual setting
- Fails to give objects when requested to do so
- Is unable to relate needs

- Echoes words and phrases or uses idiosyncratic phrases more than the average child
- May speak unusual first words, may repeat passage from movies or commercials
- Lacks understanding and/or use of nonverbal expressions
- Possesses limited range of communication functions
- May ask repetitive questions
- May develop babbling but fails to use words to refer to people or objects
- May not attend to verbal stimuli
- May show pragmatic difficulty in speech despite adequate scores on standardized tests
- Does not speak any two-word spontaneous (not just echolalia) phrases by 24 months
- Does not engage in babbling by 12 months
- Does not engage in jabbering or imitative vocalizations (9–18 months)
- Does not speak single words by 16–20 months
- Exhibits stereotyped, repetitive use of speech to satisfy own needs independently (11–19 months)
- Has unusual vocal quality and/or inflection (tone, pitch, or rate)
- Once said a few words, but now does not
- Uses and interprets language literally
- Among those who are verbal, uses speech that seems rote or like an imitation of something heard
- Uses words inconsistently and perhaps not related to needs

The Student Who Exhibits Impairments in Social Interaction

- Lacks or has a delayed social smile (1–4 months)
- Finds it difficult to engage in baby games (5–12 months)
- Encounters difficulty shifting attention appropriately
- Does not easily shift point of view/perspective
- Cannot easily shift to other topics
- Cannot sustain conversation on other topics
- Does not differentiate strangers from family
- Does not extend toys to other people
- Does not initiate
- Does not observe peers with curiosity (6–9 months)
- Does not quiet when held
- Does not seek comfort when distressed
- Does not show distress when primary caregiver leaves the room

- Does not use his or her index finger to point, to ask for something
- May avoid eye contact altogether or give only fleeting glance
- Fails to respond to mother's attention and crib toys in typical ways
- Shows impaired ability to initiate or sustain a conversation or social interaction
- Initiates conversations with a narrow range of topics; may monopolize conversation
- Interacts or relates to adults and peers in mechanical ways
- Is not interested in other students/people
- Lacks ability for associative play (36–42 months)
- Lack ability for cooperative play (42–48 months)
- Lacks ability in parallel play (20–24 months)
- Lacks social or emotional reciprocity
- Lacks varied spontaneous make-believe play or appropriate social imitative play
- Laughs, giggles, or cries inappropriately
- May appear withdrawn, aloof, standoffish
- May be socially awkward
- Makes no anticipatory social responses (6–10 months)
- Prefers to follow own agenda
- Shows more interest in objects than in people
- Engages in social interaction that is limited to a narrow range of interest and activities

The Student Who Exhibits Patterns of Behavior, Interests, and/or Activities That Are Restricted, Repetitive, or Stereotypic

- Is able to perform some difficult play or academic tasks more readily than easier ones
- Shows a compulsive adherence to routines, rituals
- Has difficulties with sequencing and planning
- Encounters difficulty shifting attention
- Finds it difficult to generalize from a "learned" context to a "novel" context
- Gets stuck on doing the same things over and exclusively focuses on one idea
- Has odd movement patterns
- Lines things up
- Possesses a literal thought process
- Does not retain previously acquired skills
- May demonstrate exceptional memory for routes, locations, or routines, but is inflexible and unable to tolerate change from what is usual

- May show emerging interest and ability with early pre-academic skills (letters and numbers) but have difficulty learning self-care skills
- May show interest in certain play repertoire but not be imaginative or flexible in a variety of play activities
- Is overly attached or preoccupied with certain objects, activities, and people
- Is physically overactive or passive
- Prefers concrete repetitive play to the exclusion of varied, spontaneous play (24–32 months)
- Is preoccupied with parts of objects
- Does not engage in pretend play; is unimaginative or repetitive
- Displays repetitive, unusual manipulation or use of toys, objects
- Seeks repetitive stimulation
- Spins objects or self
- Shows unusual interest in textures, surfaces
- Is upset by changes in the environment

The Student Who Exhibits
Unusual Responses to Sensory Information

- May show unusually long attention to self-initiated activity but very short attention to social interaction or specific skill development
- Averts gaze and reacts painfully to light, yet gazes for long periods at a visual display
- Reacts negatively and defensively to ordinary stimuli
- Has difficulty responding to textures
- Eats specific foods, refuses to eat what most people eat, or has unusual eating behaviors (e.g., will eat only one food for a period of time and then shift to something else)
- Shows inappropriate or no response to sound
- Lacks response to auditory stimuli
- Exhibits low stimulus modulation (has difficulty modifying incoming stimuli and is easily overwhelmed)
- May be described as an extremely undemanding baby who seldom cried or as a baby who was difficult to soothe
- May crave stimuli, especially proprioceptive and vestibular stimuli
- May express distress over soft touch (hair, teeth, face), clothing
- May have unusual sleep patterns
- May show unusual fear

- Possesses no understanding of danger
- Engages in persistent rocking
- Has reduced startle response
- Exhibits repetitive motor mannerisms
- Resists being cuddled or touched or seeks out "bear hugs," deep pressure activities
- Shows unusual response to or fascination with visual stimuli
- Walks on his or her toes
- May have experienced a difficult transition between food textures
- Is under- or oversensitive to certain textures, sounds, tastes, smells

Step II: Determine Procedures and Assessment Measures

If a student is suspected of having autism, use the following procedures and assessment measures:

- A developmental profile that describes the student's historical and current characteristics associated with autism
- At least three observations of the student's behavior, one of which involves direct interactions with the student
- An assessment of communication to address the communication characteristics of autism, which includes but is not limited to measures of language semantics and pragmatics completed by a speech and language pathologist
- A medical statement or a health assessment statement indicating whether any physical factors may be affecting the student's educational performance
- An assessment using an appropriate behavioral rating tool or an alternative assessment instrument that identifies characteristics associated with autism
- Additional evaluations or assessments necessary to identify the student's educational needs

A Developmental Profile That Describes the Student's Historical and Current Characteristics Associated With Autism

The evaluator must establish that the student had characteristics of ASD in early childhood. The developmental profile describes the student's historical and current characteristics associated with autism, which include

- Impairments in communication
- Impairments in social interaction
- Patterns of behavior, interests, and/or activities that are restricted, repetitive, or stereotypic
- Unusual responses to sensory information

The information must also demonstrate that the characteristics are

- Inconsistent or discrepant from the student's development in other area(s)
- Documented over time and/or intensity

Behaviors characteristic of students with ASD must be viewed relative to the student's developmental level.

At Least Three Observations of the Student's Behavior, One of Which Involves Direct Interactions With the Student

The observations should occur in multiple environments, on at least two different days, and should be completed by one or more licensed professionals knowledgeable of the behavioral characteristics of autism.

A minimum of three observations are necessary because individuals with autism may function differently under different conditions. Important environments to observe are unstructured periods (e.g., breaks, recess, lunch, free time, free play, at home), large group instruction, and structured sessions. Observations made in the course of changes in routines, interactions in the home environment, and unfamiliar environments may also help to develop an accurate picture of the student.

An Assessment of Communication to Address the Communication Characteristics of Autism, Which Includes but Is Not Limited to Measures of Language Semantics and Pragmatics Completed by a Speech and Language Pathologist

A Medical Statement or a Health Assessment Statement Indicating Whether Any Physical Factors May Be Affecting the Student's Educational Performance

The school district will send (either directly or through the parent or guardian) the health assessment form to the student's physician or physician's assistant to determine whether the team should consider any physical factor in its searsch for the underlying causes of the student's behavior. The physician may indicate there are no factors or, alternatively, may name existing factors such as mental retardation or seizures. The physician's statement may even indicate that a student has a medical diagnosis of autism. The team needs to consider any factors expressed by the physician as they complete the eligibility process. *This statement alone will not determine whether the student meets eligibility criteria for ASD*; rather, it will give needed information to the team about issues to consider as eligibility decisions are being made.

An Assessment Using an Appropriate Behavioral Rating Tool or an Alternative Assessment Instrument That Identifies Characteristics Associated With Autism

The behavioral tools identify characteristics associated with autism. They are used to help determine whether the individual student demonstrates characteristics of autism. *The score on a behavior rating tool alone does not determine eligibility for ASD.* The score and related information gained from completing the tool will provide valuable information to the team when making the eligibility determination. However, no one piece of information alone is used to determine eligibility.

Additional Evaluations or Assessments Necessary to Identify the Student's Educational Needs

The team may ask questions such as the following:

- What is reinforcing to the student?
- What does the student find aversive?
- What are the student's interest areas?

For young students, teams must identify skills needed to progress developmentally. The Individualized Family Service Plan (IFSP) reflects both the student's development and special education needs. Students with IFSPs receive specially designed educational activities in the areas of development in which they are delayed.

For school-age students, teams must identify skills needed to participate in the general curriculum. The IEP Committee's determination of how each student's disability affects the student's involvement and progress in the general curriculum is a primary consideration in developing the student's IEP. In assessing students with disabilities, school districts may use a variety of assessment techniques to determine the extent to which these students can be involved and progress in the general curriculum. These assessment techniques may include criterion-referenced tests, standard achievement tests, diagnostic tests, other tests, or any combination of the above. Thus, the IEP Committee for each student with a disability must make an individualized determination regarding how the student will be involved and progress in the general curriculum and what needs that result from the student's disability must be met to facilitate that participation.

If a student is suspected of having autism under the definition set forth in IDEA, the following assessment measures should also be considered:

- An observation by a team member other than the student's general education teacher of the student's academic performance in a general classroom setting; or in the case of a student less than school age or out of school, an observation by a team member conducted in an age-appropriate environment
- A developmental history, if needed
- An assessment of intellectual ability
- Other assessments of the characteristics of speech and language impairments if the student exhibits impairments in any one or more of the following areas: **cognition,** fine motor, perceptual motor, communication, social or emotional, and perception or memory. These assessments shall be completed by specialists knowledgeable in the specific characteristics being assessed.
- A review of cumulative records, previous IEPs or IFSPs, and teacher-collected work samples
- If deemed necessary, a medical statement or health assessment statement indicating whether any physical factors may be affecting the student's educational performance
- Assessments to determine the impact of the suspected disability on the student's educational performance (ages kindergarten–21) or on the student's developmental progress (ages 3–kindergarten)
- Additional evaluations or assessments necessary to identify the student's educational needs

Step III: Determine the
Eligibility for a Diagnosis of Autism

Autism is defined as a clinical disorder. Clinical diagnosis is made by a professional with expertise in evaluating students with a variety of behavioral and emotional disorders, including autism. Typically, student psychiatrists, clinical student psychologists, clinical neuropsychologists, and specially trained neurologists and developmental pediatricians conduct such evaluations. In addition, many professionals may administer brief **screening** tools or parent or guardian report rating scales designed to identify students who may be **at risk** of a pervasive developmental disorder, or who may show early signs of the disorder.

To receive the classification of autism, under IDEA, criteria 1 through 7 (below) should be met:

Important Point: The eligibility criteria for classifications under IDEA are not specifically stated under the law. Therefore, the eligibility criteria for a particular disability may differ from state to state. The information pertaining to "eligibility" represents the authors' professional interpretation based on reviewing the states' guidelines and criteria for autism.

1. *The student exhibits impairments in communication.* The student is unable to use expressive and receptive language for social communication in a developmentally appropriate manner, lacks nonverbal communication skills or uses abnormal nonverbal communication, uses abnormal form or content when speaking, and/or is unable to initiate or sustain conversation with others.

2. *The student exhibits difficulties in forming appropriate relationships.* The student exhibits deficits relating to people, lack of awareness of others' feelings, and abnormal seeking of comfort in times of distress; lacks social play or displays abnormal social play; and/or is unable to make friends. In addition, the student does not relate to or use objects in an age-appropriate or functional manner.

3. *The student exhibits unusual responses to sensory information.* The student has unusual, repetitive, nonmeaningful responses to auditory, visual, olfactory, taste, tactile, and/or kinesthetic stimuli.

4. *The student exhibits impairments in cognitive development.* The student has difficulty with concrete versus abstract thinking, awareness, judgment, and/or the ability to generalize. The student may exhibit perseverative thinking (e.g., staring at a spinning top for many hours) or impaired ability to process symbolic information.

5. *The student exhibits an abnormal range of activities.* The student shows a restricted repertoire of activities, interests, and imaginative development evident through stereotyped body movements, persistent preoccupation with parts of objects,

distress over trivial changes in the environment, unreasonable insistence on routines, restricted range of interests, or preoccupation with one narrow interest.

6. *The student has been previously diagnosed with autism by a qualified professional.* A licensed clinical psychologist, psychiatrist, clinical neuropsychologist, specially trained neurologist, developmental pediatrician, or other specific medical or mental health professional qualified to diagnose autism has previously diagnosed the student, accompanied by a report with recommendations for instruction.

7. *The disability (autism) is adversely affecting the student's educational performance.* The IEP Committee uses multiple sources of information to determine that educational performance is adversely affected and is not primarily due to an emotional disability.

Final Thoughts

Various conditions may be mistaken for autism and vice versa. Autism can also coexist with other disorders. It is important to carefully consider the conditions that may lead one to confuse autism with another syndrome. These conditions may include

- Mental retardation
- **Attention deficit/hyperactivity disorder (ADHD)**
- Fetal alcohol syndrome
- Obsessive compulsive disorder
- Tourette's syndrome
- Emotional disturbance

Teams need to seek out the appropriate resources to help sort the characteristics of other developmental, behavioral, and medical conditions. Resources may include both educators and medical providers specializing in, and experienced with, the various conditions. Accurate differential diagnosis is essential to avoid misleading assumptions in **remediation** plans and prognosis for the future. Differential diagnosis requires experience with a wide range of childhood developmental disorders. The team is required to consider whether the student requires special education services. Special education means specially designed instruction to meet the unique needs of the student.

3

Deaf-Blindness

Definition Under IDEA

Deaf-blindness refers to concomitant hearing and visual impairments, the combination of which causes such severe communication and other developmental and educational needs that they cannot be accommodated in special education programs solely for students with deafness or students with blindness. (34 C.F.R. 300.7(a)(c)(2))

Overview

The majority of students who have both visual and hearing impairments at birth experience major difficulties in acquiring communication and motor skills, mobility, and appropriate social skills. Because these individuals do not receive clear and consistent information from either sensory modality, they tend to turn inward to obtain the desired level of stimulation. The individual therefore may appear passive, nonresponsive, and/or noncompliant.

Students with deaf-blindness (also referred to as dual sensory impairments) may not respond to or initiate appropriate interactions with others and often exhibit behavior that is considered socially inappropriate.

Deaf-blindness is a combination of vision and hearing loss, not necessarily complete deafness and complete blindness. The thinking and developmental ability among deaf-blind individuals ranges widely from gifted to profoundly multiply handicapped. Deaf-blindness creates additional problems in the areas of mobility and communication (California Deaf-Blind Services, 1996).

Individuals who are deaf-blind need early intervention and personal attention to stimulate their understanding and interest in the world around them. The information that most students pick up naturally must be deliberately introduced to students with dual sensory impairments. Effective programs for infants and toddlers with deaf-blindness are both student- and family-centered. Student-centered approaches focus on meeting the student's individual needs, whereas a family-centered approach focuses on the student as a member of the family unit. The needs, structure, and preferences of the family will often drive the delivery of the early intervention services (Ramey & Ramey, 1999).

Communication and mobility are often the most affected areas of life for a person with deaf-blindness, causing feelings of isolation and loneliness. Development of compensatory skills can help bridge this gap. Training and instructional strategies are available to parents or guardians and educators relative to communication and mobility (California Deaf-Blind Services, 1996).

Prevalence

The population of students having deaf-blindness is small. The U.S. Department of Education (2004) reported that, during the 2003–2004 school year, 1,603 students ages 6 to 21 received special education services under the category of deaf-blindness. This accounts for less than 0.1 percent of all school-age students receiving special education services. Although relatively few students have this classification, their needs are significant and they may require substantial support and services to benefit.

Determining the Presence of Deaf-Blindness: Step by Step

Step I: Become Familiar With the Characteristics of Students With Deaf-Blindness

According to the Deaf Blind Services Division, Utah Schools for the Deaf and the Blind (n.d.), depending on the age of onset, deaf-blindness can affect learning in the areas of cognition, communication, social interaction, motor skills, and motivation.

Indicators of Deaf-Blindness

- The student has difficulty with communication.
- The student may have distorted perceptions; he or she may find it difficult to see the whole picture or to relate one element to the whole.
- The student may have difficulty anticipating what is going to happen. Clues from the environment or from the faces/actions of others may be difficult to read.
- The student may be somewhat unmotivated. Things may not be seen or heard enough to be desirable.
- The student needs to learn mainly through first-hand experiences.
- The student's lack of vision and hearing makes learning through incidental or group learning experiences difficult.
- The student has problems communicating.
- The student has problems navigating the environment.

Step II: Determine the Procedures and Assessment Measures

If a student is suspected of having deaf-blindness, an evaluation for both a visual impairment and hearing impairment should be conducted. Such evaluation should include the following:

- Evaluation by an ophthalmologist or optometrist, which documents the eye condition with the best possible correction
- A written functional vision and media assessment, completed or compiled by a licensed teacher of students with visual impairments. The assessment includes the following:
  - Observation of visual behaviors at school, home, or other environments
  - Educational implications of eye condition based on information received from eye report
  - Assessment and/or screening of expanded core curriculum skills (orientation and mobility, social interaction, visual efficiency, independent living, recreation and leisure, **career education,** assistive technology, and compensatory skills) as well as an evaluation of the student's reading and writing skills, needs, appropriate reading and writing media, and current and future needs for Braille

- School history and levels of educational performance
- Documentation and assessment of how visual impairment adversely affects educational performance in the classroom or learning environment

Evaluation for a hearing impairment should include the following:

- An audiological assessment by an audiologist licensed by a State Board of Examiners in Speech Pathology and Audiology
- A medical statement or a health assessment statement indicating whether the hearing loss, if conductive, is treatable and whether the use of **amplification** is contraindicated
- Assessments to determine the impact of the suspected disability on the student's educational performance (ages kindergarten–21) or on the student's developmental progress (ages 3–kindergarten)

Besides these assessment measures, if a student is suspected of having deaf-blindness under the definition set forth in IDEA, the following assessment measures should also be considered:

- An observation by a team member other than the student's general education teacher of the student's academic performance in a general classroom setting; or in the case of a student less than school age or out of school, an observation by a team member conducted in an age-appropriate environment
- A developmental history, if needed
- An assessment of intellectual ability
- Other assessments of the characteristics of speech and language impairments if the student exhibits impairments in any one or more of the following areas: cognition, fine motor, perceptual motor, communication, social or emotional, and perception or memory. These assessments are completed by specialists knowledgeable in the specific characteristics being assessed.
- A review of cumulative records, previous IEPs or IFSPs, and teacher-collected work samples
- If deemed necessary, a medical statement or health assessment statement indicating whether any physical factors may be affecting the student's educational performance
- Assessments to determine the impact of the suspected disability on the student's educational performance (ages kindergarten–21) or on the student's developmental progress (ages 3–kindergarten)

- Additional evaluations or assessments necessary to identify the student's educational needs

Step III: Determine Eligibility for a Diagnosis of Deaf-Blindness

For a student with deaf-blindness to be identified and determined as eligible for special education services, the IEP Committee must document that the following standards have been met:

> **Important Point:** The eligibility criteria for classifications under IDEA are not specifically stated under the law. Therefore, the eligibility criteria for a particular disability may differ from state to state. The information pertaining to "eligibility" is the authors' professional interpretation based on reviewing the states' guidelines and criteria for deaf-blindness.

- The IEP Committee has determined that the student meets the eligibility criteria for special education as a student with vision impairment; that the student meets the eligibility criteria for special education as a student with hearing impairment; or
- The student meets eligibility criteria for either hearing or vision impairment, but demonstrates inconclusive or inconsistent responses in the other sensory area. A functional assessment in the other sensory area substantiates the presence of an impairment in that area; or
- The student meets the minimum criteria for either hearing or vision impairment and has a degenerative disease or pathology that affects the acuity of the other sensory area.
- The student's disability has an adverse impact on the student's educational performance when the student is at the age of eligibility for kindergarten through age 21, or has an adverse impact on the student's developmental progress when the student is ages 3 through kindergarten.
- The student needs special education services.
- The IEP Committee has considered the student's special education eligibility and has determined that the eligibility is not due to a lack of instruction in reading or math or due to limited English proficiency.

Final Thoughts

Deaf-blindness presents a unique challenge to special educators. It requires educational approaches that are well planned and that involve many different techniques, technologies, and supportive services in order to ensure that these students have the opportunity to realize their academic, social, and vocational potential.

The services offered by schools to students with deaf-blindness need to focus on the individual needs created by each disability. Services for the deaf or hard of hearing may include

- General speech, language, and auditory training from a specialist
- Amplification systems
- Services of an interpreter for those students who use manual communication
- Favorable seating in the class to facilitate speech reading
- Captioned films/videos
- Assistance of a notetaker, who takes notes for the student with a hearing loss, so that the student can fully attend to instruction
- Instruction for the teacher and peers in alternate communication methods, such as sign language, and counseling (NEC Foundation of America, 2001)

Visual impairments should be assessed early for students to benefit from early intervention programs, when applicable. As with the deaf and hard of hearing, there is a crucial need to include assistive technology in the form of computers and low-vision optical and video aids. The introduction and use of these advanced technologies enable many partially sighted, low vision, and blind students to participate in general **mainstream** activities. Further assistance can result from the use of large-print materials, books on tape, and Braille books; FM (Frequency Modulated) trainers; and other augmentative communication devices.

The student with deaf-blindness will need additional help with special equipment and classroom and test modifications in the general curriculum to emphasize listening skills, communication, orientation and mobility, vocation/career options, and daily living skills. These students will have a greater need for an interdisciplinary approach and may require greater emphasis on self-care and daily living skills.

4

Developmental Delay

Definition Under IDEA

Students ages 3 through 9 experiencing developmental delays (DDs). The term *student with a disability* for students ages 3 through 9 may, at the discretion of the state and Local Education Agency (LEA) and in accordance with Section 300.313, include a student

- Who is experiencing DDs, as defined by the state and as measured by appropriate diagnostic instruments and procedures, in one or more of the following areas: physical development, cognitive development, communication development, social or emotional development, or adaptive development; and
- Who, by reason thereof, needs special education and related services.

Overview

The Individuals with Disabilities Education Act of 1997 (IDEA 1997) granted states the discretionary authority to establish a DD categorical option for use with young students with disabilities, beginning at age 3 and extending up through age 9.

The categorical option of DD may be used at local discretion for preschool and young students ages 3 through 9, but not beyond the age of 9. The DD option must be implemented by a local school system for preschool students with disabilities, ages 3 through 5, prior to making this option available for students beyond age 5. In addition to making the DD option available for preschool and young students, local school systems can continue to use existing disability categories established for preschool students, ages 3 through 5, as appropriate and determined by the IEP team. Any use of DD beyond age 9 is prohibited under current federal regulations.

Prevalence

According to the *Twenty-Sixth Annual Report* of the U.S. Department of Education (2004), 745,090 students between the ages of 3 and 9 were identified with the IDEA classification of DD.

Determining the Presence of a Developmental Delay: Step by Step

Step I: Become Familiar With the Characteristics of Students With Developmental Delays

To determine a student's eligibility for special education programs and/or services, there must be a significant delay or disability in the student's development. Criteria to consider when determining whether a student exhibits a delay or disability in one or more of the major areas of development are as follows:

- Delay or disability in cognitive development
- Delay or disability in language and communication
- Delay or disability in adaptive development
- Delay or disability in social-emotional development
- Delay or disability in motor development

Delay or Disability in Cognitive Development

A student with a cognitive delay or disability demonstrates deficits in intellectual abilities beyond normal variations for age and cultural background. They might include difficulties in

- The ability to acquire information
- Problem solving
- Reasoning skills
- The ability to generalize information
- Rate of learning

- Processing difficulties
- Memory delays
- Attention
- Organization skills

The factors, considerations, and observable behaviors that support or demonstrate the presence of a cognitive delay or disability are the following:

- The student has significant delays in cognitive abilities, as reflected in intellectual assessment scores, neuropsychological findings, teacher or parent or guardian rating scales, and/or results of structured observations in a classroom or other setting.
- The student shows significant discrepancies beyond what would be normally expected within or between skill development areas, such as differences between verbal and nonverbal skills, differences within verbal subareas, or differences within perceptual-motor subareas. For example, a student with good acuity to visual details may show significant deficits in problem-solving spatial skills.

Delay or Disability in Language and Communication

A student with a delay or disability in language and communication demonstrates deficits beyond normal variation for age and cultural background that adversely affect the ability to learn or acquire skills in the primary language in one or more of the following areas:

- Receptive language
- Expressive language
- **Articulation**/phonology
- Pragmatics
- Fluency
- Oral-motor skills
- Voice (such as sound quality, breath support)

The factors, considerations, and observable behaviors that support or demonstrate the presence of a language and communication delay or disability are as follows:

- The student does not use communication effectively with peers and/or adults. For example, the student does not express needs and wants in most situations.
- The student's speech and language cannot be understood by others in the student's environment who speak the same

language. This may include family members, playmates, or other students in the student's preschool program.

- The student exhibits observable severe or frequent frustration because of communication difficulties.
- The student exhibits speech sound and/or phonological process errors that impair intelligibility and are not developmentally appropriate. For example, speech sound production impairs a listener's ability to understand the student.
- The student has difficulty understanding and using age-appropriate vocabulary, language concepts, and/or conversation (e.g., limited vocabulary, sentence structure, and functional use of language restrict communication). In dual language acquisition, delays in both languages in young students are typical.
- The student demonstrates specific weaknesses in pragmatic language ability. For example, limited turn-taking, eye contact, asking and responding to questions, or knowledge of the speaker/listener role interfere with communication.
- The student demonstrates difficulty processing auditory information. For example, following simple directions or answering simple questions presents problems for the student.
- The student demonstrates oral motor difficulty, such as in swallowing or feeding, and/or developmental apraxia—the inability to coordinate speech muscle movement to say words. For example, the student has difficulty combining sounds to say words, and/or there is excessive drooling or weak oral muscle movement.
- The student demonstrates speech **dysfluency** (stuttering) that interferes with communication abilities (e.g., word sound repetitions and/or speech productions that interrupt smooth flow of speech).

Delay or Disability in Adaptive Development

A student with a delay or disability in adaptive development demonstrates difficulty learning or acquiring skills necessary for daily living and learning through play. This difficulty occurs over time, in a variety of situations, and interferes with the effectiveness of the student's ability to meet personal needs, social responsibility, or participation in developmentally appropriate situations and cultural group. **Adaptive behavior** demonstrates the effectiveness with which the individual copes with the natural and social demands of his or her environment.

Adaptive behavior areas would include activities of daily living such as toileting, eating, dressing, and personal hygiene, as well as development of play skills including the acquisition of developmentally appropriate pretend or exploratory play and engagement in peer and adult social play.

The factors, considerations, and observable behaviors that support or demonstrate the presence of an adaptive delay or disability are as follows:

- Family history, cultural factors, family expectations, and opportunities to develop self-help skills
- Motor contributions to functional skills, such as fine motor skills necessary for managing, fastening, or engaging in object exploration, oral motor components of eating, or the gross motor abilities that support environmental exploration
- The student's ability to accomplish activities of daily living adequately and as efficiently as the student's typically developing peers
- The necessity for extensive task adaptations needed to support adaptive skills that are unusual for typically developing peers (e.g., while the use of a covered cup or diaper is common for 2-year-olds, it is not expected of a 4-year-old)
- An inflexibility or rigidity in play behavior (e.g., exhibiting ritualistic self-stimulating behavior or engaging in spinning or rigid horizontal alignment of objects during free play rather than exploratory manipulation that is based on object properties)
- An avoidance of peer social interaction during play, with a preference for interaction exclusively with adults or observation of peers rather than active engagement with them during free play opportunities
- Limitations in the initiation of play activities in either independent or free play (e.g., some students will seem passive during free play, being either unaware of the play potential of a situation or afraid to engage in activities unless invited)

Delay or Disability in Social-Emotional Development

A student with a delay or disability in social-emotional development demonstrates deviations in affect or relational skills beyond normal variation for age and cultural background. These problems are exhibited over time, in various circumstances, and adversely affect the student's development of age-appropriate skills.

The factors, considerations, and observable behaviors that support or demonstrate the presence of a social-emotional delay or disability are as follows:

- The student shows significant observable behaviors such as perseveration, inability to transition, overdependence on structure and routine, and/or rigidity.
- The student exhibits significant patterns of difficulty in the following relational areas: trust building, aggressiveness, compliance, lack of age-appropriate self-control, oppositional/ defiant behavior, destructive behavior, poor awareness of self and others, or inappropriate play skills for age.

The student has significant affect difficulties such as depression/ withdrawal, limited range of emotions for a given situation, low frustration tolerance, excessive fear/anxiety, radical mood swings, and/or inappropriate fears (e.g., a student who often misinterprets the approach of other students or adults as hostile in intent).

Delay or Disability in Motor Development

A student with a delay or disability in motor development demonstrates a deficit beyond normal variability for age and experience in coordination, movement patterns, quality, or range of motion or strength and endurance of gross (large muscle), fine (small muscle), or perceptual motor (integration of sensory and motor) abilities that adversely affects the student's ability to learn or acquire skills relative to one or more of the following:

- Maintaining or controlling posture
- Functional mobility (e.g., walking or running)
- Sensory awareness of the body or movement
- Sensory integration
- Reach and/or grasp of objects
- Tool use
- Perceptual motor abilities (e.g., eye-hand coordination for tracing)
- Sequencing motor components to achieve a functional goal

The factors, considerations, and observable behaviors that support or demonstrate the presence of a delay or disability in motor development are as follows:

- The student is unable to maintain a stable posture or transition between positions (e.g., to go from standing to floor sitting) to support learning or interactive tasks.
- The student is unable to move about the environment in an efficient way that is not disruptive to others. Efficient mobility refers to both the time required for moving from one place to another and the amount of energy the student must expend to move.
- The student uses an inefficient or abnormal grasp or reach pattern that limits the ability to either explore or use objects. An inefficient grasp or reach is one that does not enable flexible manipulation, limits use of tools such as writing implements or silverware in functional tasks, leads to fatigue, or limits the student's ability to obtain or use learning materials.
- The student has problems in learning new gross and/or fine motor abilities or in using motor skills in a flexible, functional way. The student does not seem to accomplish motor tasks automatically after practice and attends to the motor aspects rather than cognitive or exploratory components of play or pre-academic programming.
- The student may achieve developmentally appropriate skills as measured on formal testing but has significant asymmetry that interferes with bilateral manipulation or tool use (e.g., the student is unable to transfer objects from hand to hand or to stabilize paper when writing or cutting).
- The student is unable to sequence one or more motor actions in order to accomplish a goal. This includes the student with clumsiness that consistently interferes with goal-directed social or object interaction.
- The student has difficulty participating in gross motor activities, is unable to complete many of the tasks performed by typically developing peers, or may refuse to participate in activities rather than seem uncoordinated.
- The student has problems in the neurological processing of information from any of the senses and organizing it for use.

Step II: Determine the Procedures and Assessment Measures

Evaluations for students for a developmental delay (for students ages 3 through 6 years) include

- The student's developmental, social, and medical history
- Vision and hearing screening of the student
- Observations in an environment natural to the student, which is completed by appropriately trained specialists familiar with student development
- Physical development assessment using standardized (norm-referenced or age-referenced), individually administered instruments in the area of total motor development (fine and gross motor combined)
- Cognitive/intellectual functioning administered by appropriate specialists using an individually administered assessment
- Language skills assessment of receptive and expressive skills combined, using norm-referenced or age-referenced instruments administered by a speech/language specialist
- Social-emotional development assessment using direct and indirect observation data compiled by an appropriate specialist
- Adaptive behavior skills assessment by an appropriately trained specialist through an appropriate standardized instrument using the student's principal caretaker and/or other familiar person (with parent or guardian consent) as an informant

Step III: Determine the Eligibility for a Diagnosis of Developmental Delay

Important Point: The eligibility criteria for classifications under IDEA are not specifically stated under the law. Therefore, the eligibility criteria for a particular disability may differ from state to state. The information pertaining to "eligibility" is the authors' professional interpretation based on reviewing the states' guidelines and criteria for DD.

An evaluation team may determine that a student is eligible for special education services as a student with a DD when all of the following criteria are met:

- An evaluation that meets the criteria has been conducted.
- The student is at least 3 years of age but less than 10 years of age.
- The student has developmental and/or learning problems that are not primarily the result of limited English proficiency, cultural difference, environmental disadvantage, or economic disadvantage.
- The student meets either of the following two criteria (a or b):
  a. The student functions at least X standard deviations below the mean (see your specific state requirements); or has a X percent delay in age equivalency (see your specific state

requirements); or functions at less than the X percentile in one or more of the following five developmental areas (see your specific state requirements): cognitive; fine motor or gross motor; speech-language (that includes articulation, fluency, voice, and receptive/expressive language); social-emotional; and self-help/adaptive.

b. The student functions at least X standard deviations below the mean (see your specific state requirements); or has a X percent delay in age equivalency (see your specific state requirements); or functions at less than the X percentile in two or more of the five developmental areas listed in (a) above (see your specific state requirements for what number is represented by X).

- The student's condition adversely affects educational performance.
- The student needs special education.

Final Thoughts

At any time a student is suspected to have a disability or DD, the student's IEP Committee reviews existing data, including information provided by the parents or guardians, instructional interventions and strategies, current classroom-based assessments, and observations by teachers and related service providers. Through a review of this information, the IEP Committee decides if additional assessments are needed to determine whether a student is experiencing a DD.

The assessment of preschool and young students should not focus on standardized diagnostic instruments, but rather on functional quantitative performance data that provides the IEP Committee, including the parents or guardians, with an accurate picture of what their student can and cannot do in the developmental areas as compared to typical developmental performance.

Local school systems *may not require* a psychological assessment for the determination of eligibility under the DD option. Based on a review of existing assessment information, and identification of areas of concern for an individual student, the IEP Committee may recommend, but not require, the administration of a formal psychological assessment. The purpose of such an assessment is to provide additional information for program planning purposes only, and not as a prerequisite for determining eligibility under this option.

5

Emotional Disturbance

Definition Under IDEA

A condition exhibiting one or more of the following characteristics over a long period of time and to a marked degree that adversely affects a student's educational performance:

(a) An inability to learn that cannot be explained by intellectual, sensory, or health factors.
(b) An inability to build or maintain satisfactory interpersonal relationships with peers and teachers.
(c) Inappropriate types of behavior or feelings under normal circumstances.
(d) A general pervasive mood of unhappiness or depression.
(e) A tendency to develop physical symptoms or fears associated with personal or school problems.

The term includes schizophrenia. The term does not apply to students who are socially maladjusted, unless it is determined that they have an emotional disturbance. (34 C.F.R. 300.7(a)(c)(4)(i))

Overview

The term *emotional disturbance* is often used interchangeably with the terms *emotional disorder/problem, behavior disorder/disturbance, psychiatric illness,* and *mental illness/disorder.* An emotional disturbance refers to social, emotional, or behavioral functioning that so deviates from generally accepted, age-appropriate ethnic or cultural norms that it adversely affects a student's academic progress, social relationships, personal adjustment, classroom adjustment, self-care, or vocational skills.

The causes of emotional disturbance have not been adequately determined. Biological factors, environment, or a mix of the two can cause mental health problems in youth. Examples of biological causes are genetics, chemical imbalances in the body, and damage to the central nervous system, such as head injury. Among the many environmental factors that can put students at risk of developing mental health problems are exposure to violence, stress-related chronic poverty, discrimination, and other hardships or loss of important people in their lives through death, divorce, or broken relationships. Although various factors such as heredity, brain disorder, diet, stress, and family functioning have been suggested as possible causes, research has not shown any of these factors to be the direct cause of behavior or emotional problems (Jensen, 2005).

Students with the most serious emotional disturbances may exhibit distorted thinking, excessive anxiety, bizarre motor acts, and abnormal mood swings. Some are identified as students who have a severe psychosis or schizophrenia (Jensen, 2005).

Many students who do not have emotional disturbances may display some of these same behaviors at various times during their development. Only when students exhibit these behaviors continuously over long periods of time, however, are they considered to be suffering from emotional disturbances. Their behaviors thus signal that they are not coping with their environment or peers (Turnbull, Turnbull, Shank, & Smith, 2004).

Possibly more than any other group of students with disabilities, students with emotional or behavior disorders present problems to themselves, their families, their peers, and their teachers (U.S. Department of Education, 2001).

Prevalence

According to the *Twenty-Sixth Annual Report* of the U.S. Department of Education (2004), 482,597 students between the ages of 6 and 21 were identified as having emotional disturbances. This represents slightly more than 8 percent of all students who are classified as special education students, or less than 1 percent of all school-age students.

Determining the Presence of an Emotional Disturbance: Step by Step

Step I: Become Familiar With the Characteristics of Students With Emotional/Behavioral Disorders

The characteristics often associated with students having emotional and/or behavioral disorders include

- An inability to build or maintain satisfactory interpersonal relationships with peers and teachers, as evidenced in the following behaviors:
    - Physical or verbal aggression when others approach the students
    - Lack of affect or disorganized/distorted emotions toward others
    - Demands for constant attention from others
    - Withdrawal from all social interactions
- Inappropriate types of behavior or feelings under normal circumstances, as shown by
    - Limited or excessive self-control
    - Low frustration tolerance, emotional overreactions, and **impulsivity**
    - Limited premeditation or planning
    - Limited ability to predict consequences of behavior
    - Rapid changes in behavior or mood
    - Antisocial behaviors
    - Excessive dependence and over-closeness, and/or inappropriate rebellion and defiance; and low self-esteem and/or distorted self-concept
- A general pervasive mood of unhappiness or depression, including
    - Depressed or irritable mood most of the time (e.g., feeling sad, appearing tearful)
    - Diminished interest or pleasure in daily activities
    - Significant and unexpected changes in weight or appetite
    - Insomnia or hypersomnia nearly every day
    - Fatigue or diminished energy nearly every day
    - Feelings of worthlessness or excessive or inappropriate guilt
    - Diminished ability to think or concentrate, or indecisiveness, nearly every day
    - Recurrent thoughts of death, or suicidal ideation

- Physical symptoms or fears associated with the student's personal or school life, such as
  - Headaches
  - Gastrointestinal problems
  - Cardiopulmonary symptoms
  - Incapacitating feelings of anxiety often accompanied by trembling, hyperventilating, and/or dizziness
  - Panic attacks characterized by physical symptoms, precipitated, for example, when an object, activity, individual, or situation cannot be avoided or is confronted
  - Persistent and irrational fears of particular objects or situations
  - Intense fears or irrational thoughts related to separation from parents or guardians
- Other characteristics of students with emotional disturbance include
  - A lack of understanding about the consequences of actions
  - Problems with reasoning characterized by confused thoughts about and perceptions of social situations
  - Highly unusual and bizarre behaviors
  - A lack of understanding or misinterpretations of social conventions and behavioral expectations
  - Excessive anxiety, pervasive depression, and/or excessive guilt

As suggested earlier, an emotional disturbance exists only when the traits are considered to have been exhibited over a long period of time and to a marked degree. That is, the characteristic(s) are persistent, generalized, and extended over time and situations. The marked degree standard is met when the characteristic(s) are significantly deviant from expectations for age-level peers and have a low-frequency occurrence in the peer group.

Step II: Determine the Procedures and Assessment Measures

Each student is given a multidisciplinary evaluation for the initial assessment of a suspected disability (emotional disturbance) that includes, but is not limited to, the following:

- Comprehensive social history collected directly from the student's parent or guardian; custodial guardian; or, if necessary, an individual with intimate knowledge of the student's circumstances, history, or current behaviors. A comprehensive social assessment includes family history, family-social interactions, developmental history, medical history (including mental health), and school history (including attendance and discipline records).

- Direct and **anecdotal** observations over time and across various settings by three or more licensed professionals
- Documentation and assessment of how the emotional disturbance adversely affects educational performance in the learning environment
- Individual assessment of psychoeducational strengths and weaknesses, including intelligence, behavior, and personality factors, taking into account any exceptionality of the individual in the choice of assessment procedures
- Individual educational assessment (criterion- or norm-referenced), including direct measures of classroom performance to determine the student's strengths and weaknesses
- Physical conditions ruled out as the primary cause of atypical behavior(s)
- Review of past educational performance
- Specific behavioral data, including documentation of previous interventions and an evaluation of the locus of control of behavior to include internal and external factors
- Visual or auditory deficits ruled out as the primary cause of atypical behavior(s)

If a student is suspected of having an emotional disturbance under the definition set forth in IDEA, the following assessment measures should also be considered:

- An observation by a team member other than the student's general education teacher of the student's academic performance in a general classroom setting; or in the case of a student less than school age or out of school, an observation by a team member conducted in an age-appropriate environment
- A developmental history, if needed
- An assessment of intellectual ability
- Other assessments of the characteristics of speech and language impairments if the student exhibits impairments in any one or more of the following areas: cognition, fine motor, perceptual motor, communication, social or emotional, and perception or memory. These assessments are to be completed by specialists knowledgeable in the specific characteristics being assessed.
- A review of cumulative records, previous IEPs or IFSPs, and teacher-collected work samples

- If deemed necessary, a medical statement or health assessment statement indicating whether any physical factors may be affecting the student's educational performance
- Assessments to determine the impact of the suspected disability on the student's educational performance (ages kindergarten–21) or on the student's developmental progress (ages 3–kindergarten)
- Additional evaluations or assessments as necessary to identify the student's educational needs

Step III: Determine the Eligibility for a Diagnosis of an Emotional Disturbance

Important Point: The eligibility criteria for classifications under IDEA are not specifically stated under the law. Therefore, the eligibility criteria for a particular disability may differ from state to state. The information pertaining to "eligibility" is the authors' professional interpretation based on reviewing the states' guidelines and criteria for emotional disturbance.

To be eligible for a classification as a student with an emotional disturbance under IDEA, the following standards should be met:

Determine Whether the Student Exhibits One or More of the Following

- *An inability to learn at a rate commensurate with the student's intellectual, sensory motor, and physical development.* This characteristic requires documentation that a student is not able to learn, despite appropriate instructional strategies and/or support services. A comprehensive and differential assessment is performed to establish an "inability to learn." The assessment should rule out any other primary reasons for the suspected disability, such as mental retardation, speech and language disorders, autism, learning disability, hearing/vision impairment, multihandicapping conditions, traumatic brain injury, neurological impairment, or other medical condition. If any of these other conditions is the primary cause, then the student may be deemed eligible for special education under that category of disability; OR
- *An inability to build or maintain satisfactory interpersonal relationships with peers and teachers.* This characteristic requires documentation that the student is unable to initiate or to maintain satisfactory interpersonal relationships with peers and teachers. Satisfactory interpersonal relationships include the ability to demonstrate sympathy, warmth, and empathy toward

others; establish and maintain friendships; be constructively assertive; and work and play independently. These abilities should be considered when observing the student's interactions with both peers and teachers. This characteristic does not refer to the student who has conflict with only one teacher or with certain peers. Rather, it is a pervasive inability to develop relationships with others across settings and situations; OR

- *Inappropriate types of behavior or feelings under normal circumstances.* This characteristic requires documentation that the student's inappropriate behavior or feelings deviate significantly from expectations for the student's age, gender, and culture across different environments. The IEP Committee must determine whether the student's inappropriate responses are occurring "under normal circumstances." When considering "normal circumstances," the IEP Committee should take into account whether a student's home or school situation is disrupted by stress, recent changes, or unexpected events; OR

- *A general pervasive mood of unhappiness or depression.* This characteristic requires documentation that the student's unhappiness or depression is occurring across most, if not all, of the student's life situations. The student must demonstrate a consistent pattern of depression or unhappiness in keeping with the criterion "long period of time" (i.e., several months). In other words, this pattern is not a temporary response to situational factors or to a medical condition.

The characteristics should not be a secondary manifestation attributable to substance abuse, medication, or a general medical condition (e.g., hypothyroidism). The characteristics cannot be the effect of normal bereavement; OR

- *Physical symptoms or fears associated with the student's personal or school life.* Physical symptoms that qualify under the emotional disturbance characteristic should adhere to the following four conditions:
  1. Symptoms suggesting physical disorders are present with no demonstrable medical findings.
  2. Positive evidence or strong presumption exists that these symptoms are linked to psychological factors/conflict.
  3. The person is not conscious of intentionally producing the symptoms.
  4. The symptoms are not a culturally sanctioned response pattern.

Determine Whether the Student's Educational Performance Is Adversely Affected

Indicators of educational performance include present and past grades, achievement test scores, and measures of ongoing classroom performance (e.g., curriculum-based assessment and work samples). Adverse effect on educational performance implies a marked difference between the student's academic performance and reasonable (not optimal) expectations of performance. The appropriateness of the school district's educational goals, as reflected in the curriculum and in the formal grading report, should be considered in determining whether the student's performance meets reasonable expectations.

Determine That the Student Does Not Meet the Criteria for a "Socially Maladjusted" Student

A social maladjustment is a persistent pattern of violating societal norms, such as multiple acts of truancy or substance or sex abuse, and is marked by struggle with authority, low frustration threshold, impulsivity, or manipulative behaviors. A social maladjustment unaccompanied by an emotional disturbance is often indicated by some or all of the following:

- Unhappiness or depression is not pervasive.
- Problem behaviors are goal-directed, self-serving, and manipulative.
- Actions are based on perceived self-interest even though others may consider the behavior to be self-defeating.
- General social conventions and behavioral standards are understood but not accepted.
- Problem behaviors have escalated during preadolescence or adolescence.
- Inappropriate behaviors are displayed in selected settings or situations (e.g., only at home, in school, or in selected classes), while other behavior is appropriately controlled.
- Problem behaviors are frequently the result of encouragement by a peer group, are intentional, and the student understands the consequences of such behaviors.

Final Thoughts

Assessment information collected or generated during the eligibility determination phase should contribute to developing the plan that eventually becomes the IEP. These assessments by the multidisciplinary evaluation team should yield a profile of the student's needs and strengths as well as the student's characteristic pattern of response to environmental and internal influences. Assessment for serious emotional disturbance will include not only information about the student's aptitude and academic achievement levels but also information regarding (1) social and personal competence needed to maximize independence and, (2) when appropriate, the student's vocational aptitudes and interests. Social and personal information should lead to the identification of affective skills to be targeted in the IEP. Examples include (1) managing anger, frustration, and other emotions that tend to exacerbate conflict with peers, teachers, and school administrators and (2) coping effectively with withdrawal or depression.

The IEP Committee may not identify or may refuse to identify a student as having an emotional behavioral disability solely on the basis that the student has another disability or is socially maladjusted, an adjudged delinquent, a dropout, or chemically dependent; or because a student's behavior is primarily due to cultural deprivation, familial instability, suspected student abuse or socioeconomic circumstances; or when medical or psychiatric diagnostic statements have been used to describe the student's behavior.

6

Hearing Impairment

Definition Under IDEA

IDEA includes "hearing impairment" and "deafness" as two of the categories under which students with disabilities may be eligible for special education and related services programming. While the term *hearing impairment* is often used generically to describe a wide range of hearing losses, including deafness and hard-of-hearing, the regulations for IDEA define hearing loss and deafness separately.

Under the federal law, IDEA defines a hearing impairment as *an impairment in hearing, whether permanent or fluctuating, that adversely affects a student's educational performance*. It defines deafness as *a hearing impairment that is so severe that the student is impaired in processing linguistic information through hearing, with or without amplification.* (34 C.F.R. 300.7(a)(c)(5))

Overview

Deafness and hearing loss may be defined according to the degree of hearing impairment, which is determined by assessing an individual's sensitivity to loudness (sound intensity) and pitch (sound frequency). Sound is measured by its loudness or intensity (measured in units called decibels, dB) and its frequency or pitch (measured in units called hertz, Hz). The range of human hearing is approximately 0 to 130 dB.

Impairments in hearing can occur in either or both areas and may exist in only one ear or in both ears. Hearing loss is generally described as slight, mild, moderate, severe, or profound, depending on how well a person can hear the intensities or frequencies most greatly associated with speech. Generally, only students whose hearing loss is greater than 90 dB are considered deaf for the purposes of educational placement (Hardman, Drew, & Egan, 2005).

According to the National Dissemination Center for Children with Disabilities (2004a), there are four different types of hearing loss:

1. Conductive hearing losses are due to the effects of diseases or obstructions in the outer or middle ear (the conduction pathways for sound to reach the inner ear). Conductive hearing losses usually affect all frequencies of hearing evenly and do not result in severe losses. A person with a conductive hearing loss usually is able to use a hearing aid well or can be helped medically or surgically.

2. Sensorineural hearing losses result from damage to the delicate sensory hair cells of the inner ear or the nerves that supply it. These hearing losses can range from mild to profound. They often affect the person's ability to hear certain frequencies more than others. Thus, even with amplification to increase the sound level, a person with a sensorineural hearing loss may perceive distorted sounds, sometimes making the successful use of a hearing aid impossible.

3. Mixed hearing losses refer to a combination of conductive and sensorineural loss and means that a problem occurs in both the outer or middle and the inner ear.

4. Central hearing losses result from damage or impairment to the nerves or nuclei of the central nervous system, either in the pathways to the brain or in the brain itself.

Prevalence

According to the *Twenty-Sixth Annual Report* of the U.S. Department of Education (2004), during the 2003–2004 school year, 71,118 students ages 6 to 21 (or 1.2 percent of all students with disabilities) received special education services under the category of "Hearing

Impairment." However, the number of students with hearing loss and deafness is undoubtedly higher, since many of these students may have other disabilities as well and may be served under other categories (Holden-Pitt & Diaz, 1998). Also, these figures only represent those students who receive special services; a number of students with hearing loss who could benefit from additional services do not receive them (U.S. Department of Education, 2004; cited in Heward, 2006).

Determining the Presence of a Hearing Impairment: Step by Step

Step I: Become Familiar With the Characteristics of Students With Hearing Impairments

Behaviors That May Indicate a Hearing Impairment

The student with a hearing impairment

- Gives no response when spoken to
- Often gives irrelevant or incorrect responses to questions
- Seems unable to follow spoken directions to carry out an activity
- Often says, "huh?" or "what?" and requires repetition
- Seems unaware that others are talking and interrupts conversations
- Seems to have a behavioral problem or is irritable
- Expresses confusion or uncertainty when unable to understand
- Holds head in an abnormal position to listen "better"; seems unable to locate the source of sound
- Watches a speaker's face intently
- Seem inattentive but pays more attention to visual things
- Speaks more loudly or softly than expected for a situation; has an unusual vocal tone, resonance, or pattern of speaking
- Makes greater use of gestures and objects to get attention than would be expected
- Seems to have language problems (structure, syntax, and vocabulary)
- Seems to withdraw from interaction in groups
- Has frequent colds, earaches or ear infections, and allergies
- Breathes more through the mouth than through the nose
- Complains or shows signs of ear pain, fullness in the ear, dizziness, or balance problems

Step II: Determine the Procedures and Assessment Measures

If a student is suspected of having a hearing impairment, the following evaluation shall be conducted:

- An audiological assessment by an audiologist licensed by a State Board of Examiners in Speech Pathology and Audiology
- A medical statement or a health assessment statement indicating whether the hearing loss, if conductive, is treatable and whether the use of amplification is contraindicated
- Assessments to determine the impact of the suspected disability on the student's educational performance (ages kindergarten–21) or on the student's developmental progress (ages 3–kindergarten)
- Additional evaluations or assessments necessary to identify the student's educational needs

Besides these assessment measures, if a student is suspected of having a hearing impairment under the definition set forth in IDEA, the following assessment measures should also be considered:

- An observation by a team member other than the student's general education teacher of the student's academic performance in a general classroom setting; or in the case of a student less than school age or out of school, an observation by a team member conducted in an age-appropriate environment
- A developmental history, if needed
- An assessment of intellectual ability
- Other assessments of the characteristics of speech and language impairments if the student exhibits impairments in any one or more of the following areas: cognition, fine motor, perceptual motor, communication, social or emotional, and perception or memory. These assessments are to be completed by specialists knowledgeable in the specific characteristics being assessed.
- A review of cumulative records, previous IEPs or IFSPs, and teacher-collected work samples
- If deemed necessary, a medical statement or health assessment statement indicating whether any physical factors may be affecting the student's educational performance
- Assessments to determine the impact of the suspected disability on the student's educational performance (ages

kindergarten–21) or on the student's developmental progress (ages 3–kindergarten)

- Additional evaluations or assessments necessary to identify the student's educational needs

Step III: Determine the Eligibility for a Diagnosis of a Hearing Impairment

For a student suspected of having a hearing impairment, determine that the student shall meet one of the following minimum criteria:

> **Important Point:** The eligibility criteria for classifications under IDEA are not specifically stated under the law. Therefore, the eligibility criteria for a particular disability may differ from state to state. The information pertaining to "eligibility" is the authors' professional interpretation based on reviewing the states' guidelines and criteria for hearing impairments.

- The student has a pure tone average loss of 25 dbHL or greater in the better ear for frequencies of 500 Hz, 1,000 Hz, and 2,000 Hz, or a pure tone average loss of 35 dbHL or greater in the better ear for frequencies of 3,000 Hz, 4,000 Hz, and 6,000 Hz.
- The student has a unilateral hearing impairment with a pure tone average loss of 50 dbHL or greater in the affected ear for the frequencies 500 Hz to 4,000 Hz.
- The loss is either sensorineural or conductive if the conductive loss has been determined to be currently untreatable by a physician.

For a student to be eligible for special education services as a student with a hearing impairment, determine that the student's disability has an adverse impact on the student's educational performance (ages kindergarten–21) or on the student's developmental progress (ages 3–kindergarten).

Determine that the student needs special education services as a result of the disability.

Final Thoughts

For babies who are born deaf or diagnosed with a hearing impairment, the earliest possible detection and intervention are crucial. Currently, a student's hearing loss is usually diagnosed between the ages of 14 months and 3 years—resulting in the loss of a significant window of opportunity for acquiring language, whether spoken or signed. A delayed diagnosis can also affect a student's social skills. Ultimately, the research strongly suggests that students with a hearing loss must receive early intervention as soon as possible if they are to learn the language skills necessary for reading and other academic subjects as they approach the school years (Calderon & Naidu, 2000).

7

Specific Learning Disabilities

Definition Under IDEA

(i) General. The term means a disorder in one or more of the basic psychological processes involved in understanding or in using language, spoken or written, that may manifest itself in an imperfect ability to listen, think, speak, read, write, spell, or to do mathematical calculations, including conditions such as perceptual disabilities, brain injury, minimal brain dysfunction, **dyslexia,** *and developmental* **aphasia.**

(ii) Disorders not included. The term does not include learning problems that are primarily the result of visual, hearing, or motor disabilities, of mental retardation, of emotional disturbance, or of environmental, cultural, or economic disadvantage. (34 C.F.R. 300.7(c)(10))

Important Point: The definition of "a specific learning disability" under IDEA 2004 remains unchanged from IDEA of 1997. However, under the new provisions under IDEA 2004, *a local educational agency is not required to take into consideration whether a student has a severe discrepancy between achievement and intellectual ability in oral expression, listening comprehension, written expression, basic reading skill, reading comprehension, mathematical calculation or mathematical reasoning. In determining whether a student has a specific learning disability, a local educational agency may use a process that determines if a student responds to scientific, research-based intervention as a part of the evaluation procedures.* (U.S.C. sec. 614(b)(2)(3))

Overview

In general, the term *learning disabilities* refers to a neurobiological disorder related to differences in how one's brain works and is structured. It also describes specific kinds of learning problems. A learning disability can cause a person to have trouble learning and using certain skills (Lerner, 2003). The skills most often affected are reading, writing, listening, speaking, reasoning, and doing math (Heward, 2006; National Dissemination Center for Children with Disabilities, 2004b; Pierangelo & Giuliani, 2006b).

The National Joint Committee on Learning Disabilities (NJCLD) discusses the following five constructs underlying the definition of learning disabilities:

1. Learning disabilities are heterogeneous, both within and across individuals. Intraindividual differences involve varied profiles of learning strength and need and/or shifts across the life span within individuals, whereas interindividual differences involve different manifestations of learning disabilities for different individuals.

2. Learning disabilities result in significant difficulties in the acquisition and use of listening, speaking, reading, writing, reasoning, and/or mathematical skills. Such difficulties are evident when an individual's appropriate levels of effort do not result in reasonable progress given the opportunity for effective educational instruction and with the recognition that all individuals learn at a different pace and with differing effort. Significant difficulty cannot be determined solely by a quantitative test score.

3. Learning disabilities are intrinsic to the individual. They are presumed to be related to differences in central nervous system development. They do not disappear over time, but may range in expression and severity at different life stages.

4. Learning disabilities may occur concomitantly with other disabilities that do not, by themselves, constitute a learning disability. For example, difficulty with self-regulatory behaviors, social perception, and social interactions may occur for many reasons. Some social interaction problems result from learning disabilities; others do not. Individuals with other disabilities, such as sensory impairments, ADHD, mental retardation, and serious emotional disturbance, may also have learning disabilities, but such conditions do not cause or constitute learning disabilities.

5. Learning disabilities are not caused by extrinsic influences. Inconsistent or insufficient instruction or a lack of instructional experience causes learning difficulties but not learning disabilities. However, individuals who have had inconsistent or insufficient instruction may also have learning disabilities. The challenge is to document the notion that inadequate or insufficient instruction is not the primary cause of a learning disability. Individuals from all cultural and linguistic backgrounds may also have learning disabilities; therefore, assessments must be designed acknowledging this diversity in culture and language, and examiners who test students from each background must be sensitive to such factors and use practices that are individualized and appropriate for each student.

Prevalence

According to the *Twenty-Sixth Annual Report* of the U.S. Department of Education (2004), 2,816,361 students between the ages of 6 and 21 were identified as having specific learning disabilities (SLDs). This represents approximately 47 percent of all students having a classification in special education, or about 5 percent of all school-age students.

Determining the Presence of a Specific Learning Disability: Step by Step

Step I: Become Familiar With the Characteristics of Students With Specific Learning Disabilities

No one sign indicates that a person has a learning disability. Experts look for a noticeable difference between how well a student does in school and how well he or she *could* do, given his or her intelligence or ability. There are also certain clues that may mean a student has a learning disability. Most relate to elementary school tasks because learning disabilities tend to be identified in elementary school. A student probably will not show all of these signs, or even most of them. However, if a student shows a number of these problems, then parents or guardians and the teacher should consider the possibility that the student has a learning disability.

When a student has a learning disability, he or she

- May have trouble learning the alphabet, rhyming words, or connecting letters to their sounds

- May make many mistakes when reading aloud, and repeat and pause often
- May not understand what he or she reads
- May have real trouble with spelling
- May have very messy handwriting or hold a pencil awkwardly
- May struggle to express ideas in writing
- May learn language late and have a limited vocabulary
- May have trouble remembering the sounds that letters make or hearing slight differences between words
- May have trouble understanding jokes, comic strips, and sarcasm
- May have trouble following directions
- May mispronounce words or use a wrong word that sounds similar
- May have trouble organizing what he or she wants to say or not be able to think of the word he or she needs for writing or conversation
- May not follow the social rules of conversation, such as taking turns, and may stand too close to the listener
- May confuse math symbols and misread numbers
- May not be able to retell a story in order (what happened first, second, third)
- May not know where to begin a task or how to go on from there

If a student has unexpected problems learning to read, write, listen, speak, or do math, then teachers and parents or guardians may want to investigate further. The same is true if the student is struggling to learn any one of these skills. The student may need to be evaluated to see if he or she has a learning disability.

Step II: Determine the Procedures and Assessment Measures

If a student is suspected of having a specific learning disability, the following evaluation should be considered:

- An observation by a team member other than the student's general education teacher of the student's academic performance in a general classroom setting; or in the case of a student less than school age or out of school, an observation by a team member conducted in an age-appropriate environment
- A developmental history, if needed

- An assessment of intellectual ability
- Other assessments of the characteristics of learning disabilities if the student exhibits impairments in any one or more of the following areas: cognition, fine motor, perceptual motor, communication, social or emotional, and perception or memory. These assessments shall be completed by specialists knowledgeable in the specific characteristics being assessed.
- A review of cumulative records, previous IEPs or IFSPs, and teacher-collected work samples
- If deemed necessary, a medical statement or health assessment statement indicating whether any physical factors may be affecting the student's educational performance
- Assessments to determine the impact of the suspected disability on the student's educational performance (ages kindergarten–21) or on the student's developmental progress (ages 3–kindergarten)
- Additional evaluations or assessments necessary to identify the student's educational needs

At least one observation is required as part of the evaluation for determining a specific learning disability. Minimal observation requirements include the following:

- At least one team member other than the student's general education teacher should observe the student's academic performance in the general classroom setting. In the case of a student less than school age or out of school, a team member observes the student in an environment appropriate for a student of that age.
- The relevant behavior of the student should be noted during the observation of that student, and the relationship of that behavior to the student's academic functioning should be documented.

You also need documentation that the student's learning problems are not primarily due to

- Lack of appropriate instruction in reading and math
- Limited English proficiency
- Visual, hearing, or motor impairment
- Mental retardation

- Emotional disturbance
- Environmental, cultural, or economic disadvantage
- Motivational factors
- Situational traumas

Step III: Determine the Eligibility for a Diagnosis of a Specific Learning Disability

Important Point: The eligibility criteria for classifications under IDEA are not specifically stated under the law. Therefore, the eligibility criteria for a particular disability may differ from state to state. The information pertaining to "eligibility" is the authors' professional interpretation based on reviewing the states' guidelines and criteria for specific learning disabilities.

In general, states use two different methods to determine whether a student meets the eligibility criteria as a student with a specific learning disability under IDEA. We present a synopsis of these two options for an IEP Committee to consider.

Option 1

To identify and be determined as eligible for special education services as a student with a specific learning disability, the IEP Committee documents that the following standards have been met. Based on the results of the assessment,

- The student demonstrates a continued lack of progress when provided with appropriate instruction in the suspected area of disability.
- Documented evidence exists indicating that effective general education interventions and strategies have been attempted over a reasonable period of time.
- The determining factor for identifying a learning disability is not due to a lack of appropriate instruction in reading and math.
- Evidence exists that the student does not achieve commensurate with his or her age and ability in one or more of the following areas: listening comprehension, oral expression, basic reading skills, reading comprehension, written expression, mathematics calculation, and/or mathematics reasoning.
- There is a severe discrepancy between educational performance and predicted achievement that is based on the best measure of cognitive ability. (This is an *optional consideration* under IDEA 2004.) Cognitive ability/achievement discrepancies should be used cautiously because a learning disability can exist when a numerical discrepancy does not. Such comparisons may assist in

the diagnostic process. Careful diagnosticians examine all information and recognize developmental factors, including age and academic experience, in making a determination as to the value of such discrepancies.

- There is evidence of a cognitive processing disorder that adversely affects the student's academic achievement. A cognitive processing disorder is defined as a deficit in the manner in which a student receives, stores, transforms, retrieves, and expresses information. Documented evidence exists that demonstrates or expresses the manifestation of the processing disorder in the identified achievement deficit.

- Evidence exists that the student's learning problems are not due primarily to visual, hearing, or motor impairments; mental retardation; emotional disturbance; environmental, cultural, or economic disadvantage; limited English proficiency; motivational factors; or situational traumas.

- There is evidence that characteristics as defined above are present and that the severity of the student's specific learning disability adversely affects his or her progress in the general education curriculum, demonstrating the need for special education and related services, and that students who perform in classroom academics in a manner commensurate with expected academic standards at the student's grade level cannot be considered as having a specific learning disability, even though they may show deficits on achievement tests in one or more academic areas.

Option 2

The team determines that a student has a specific learning disability and is in need of special education and related services when the pupil meets the criteria described in items 1 through 3 that follow. Information about each item must be sought from the parent or guardian and included as part of the assessment data. The assessment data must confirm that the disabling effects of the student's disability occur in a variety of settings:

- The student must demonstrate severe **underachievement** in response to usual classroom instruction. The performance measures used to verify this finding must be both representative of the student's curriculum and useful for developing instructional goals and objectives. The following assessment procedures are required at a minimum to verify this finding:

  – Evidence of low achievement from sources such as cumula-
    tive record reviews, classwork samples, anecdotal teacher
    records, formal and informal tests, curriculum-based assess-
    ment results
  – Observation of the student's academic performance in the
    general classroom setting by at least one team member
    other than the student's general education teacher. In the
    case of a student served through an Early Childhood Special
    Education program or who is out of school, a team member
    observes the student in an environment appropriate for a
    student of that age.
• The student must demonstrate a severe discrepancy between
  general intellectual ability and achievement in one or more of
  the following areas: oral expression, listening comprehension,
  written expression, basic reading skills, reading comprehension, mathematical calculation, or mathematical reasoning. The
  demonstration of a severe discrepancy cannot be based solely on
  the use of standardized tests. The team considers these standardized test results as only one component of the eligibility criteria.
  – The instruments used to assess the student's general intellec-
    tual ability and achievement must be individually adminis-
    tered and interpreted by an appropriately licensed person
    using standardized procedures.
  – For initial placement, the severe discrepancy must be equal
    to or greater than 1.75 standard deviations below the mean of
    the distribution of difference scores for the general popula-
    tion of individuals at the student's chronological age level.
• The team must agree that it has sufficient assessment data that
  verify the following conclusions:
  – The student has an information processing condition that is
    manifested by such behaviors as inadequate or lack of orga-
    nizational skills (such as in following directions, written and
    oral; spatial arrangements; correct use of developmental
    order in relating events; transfer of information onto paper),
    memory (visual and auditory), expression (verbal and non-
    verbal), and motor control for written tasks such as pencil
    and paper assignments, drawing, and copying.
  – The disabling effects of the student's information processing
    condition occur in a variety of settings.
  – The student's underachievement is not primarily the result
    of vision, hearing, or motor impairment; mental impairment;
    emotional or behavioral disorders; environmental, cultural,

or economic influences; or a history of an inconsistent education program.

Response to Intervention (RTI)

Before students can be eligible for special education services, research-based interventions must be utilized based on IDEA. According to the NJCLD (2005), **Response to Intervention, or RTI,** is the practice of

- Providing high-quality instruction/intervention matched to student needs
- Using learning rate over time and level of performance to make important educational decisions

Although there is no single, widely used "model" for RTI, it is generally defined as a three-tier model that uses research-based interventions designed to help a student become more successful, rather than focusing on the student's lack of success.

The whole idea of RTI is to prevent students from developing more serious academic and behavior problems. The earlier we catch potential problems, the better chance the students have to be successful.

A key element of an RTI approach is the provision of early intervention when students first experience academic difficulties, with the goal of improving the achievement of all students, including those who may have specific learning disabilities. In addition to the preventive and remedial services this approach may provide to at-risk students, it holds promise for contributing data useful for identifying SLD. Thus, a student exhibiting (1) significantly low achievement and (2) insufficient RTI may be regarded as being at risk for learning disabilities and, in turn, as possibly in need of special education and related services. The assumption behind this paradigm, which has been referred to as a dual discrepancy (Fuchs, Fuchs, & Speece, 2002) by least one team member other than the student's general education teacher, is that when provided with quality instruction and remedial services, a student without disabilities will make satisfactory progress.

Final Thoughts

Ongoing assessment throughout the school years is critical to develop the educational potential of all students, especially those with learning disabilities. School personnel, parents or guardians, and students should proceed with as much information as possible, giving consideration to individual skills and academic needs.

The recent explosion in brain research is beginning to impact teaching practice and address the differences in brain anatomy and chemistry in students with SLD. Some current findings include insights on causation, hemispheric functioning, writing dysfunctions, dyslexia, and laterality. Overall, scientific support has been found for some LD characteristics that were previously identified mainly through observation and testing. Other information found in these studies suggests that learning disabilities teachers need to change some teaching practices based on brain research. As time goes on, there will be advances in identifying even more patterns of thinking in students with learning disabilities.

Given the enormous variability in the population of students with learning disabilities, the proliferation of tests on the market, and the problems inherent in applying the definition, it has been extremely difficult to identify specific assessment instruments that consistently and appropriately identify these students. The problem of distinguishing students with learning disabilities from students without this handicap has become even more compounded by recent research suggesting that poor readers without disabilities and students who have been identified with mild learning disabilities may not differ significantly in the areas of information processing, genetic, or neurophysiological characteristics.

8

Mental Retardation

Definition Under IDEA

According to IDEA, mental retardation is defined as *significantly subaverage general intellectual functioning, existing concurrently with deficits in adaptive behavior and manifested during the developmental period, that adversely affects a student's educational performance.* (34 C.F.R. 300.7 (a)(c)(6))

Overview

The term *mental retardation* describes certain limitations in a person's mental functioning and in skills such as communicating, taking care of self, and social skills. These limitations will cause a student to learn and develop more slowly than a typical student. Students with mental retardation may take longer to learn to speak, walk, and take care of their personal needs such as dressing or eating. They are likely to have trouble learning in school; although they will learn, it will take them longer. Those with mental retardation may not be able to learn some concepts (National Dissemination Center for Children with Disabilities, 2004c). Today, the field of mental retardation continues to evolve with an emphasis on inclusive practices, recommended strategies, and decreasing the stigma for those diagnosed with mental retardation.

Over the past decade, several efforts have been made to describe mental retardation in terms of needed levels of support rather than in terms of deficits. Efforts have also been made to shift from the term *mental retardation* to *intellectual disability* (ID), which more accurately connotes the cognitive underpinning of the disability.

ID can be viewed as a disorder in three distinct areas: thinking (conceptual), learning (practical), and social competence. Students with ID show more limitations in the spontaneous use of thinking skills that will enable them to learn effectively. These students encounter difficulty when they have to make decisions about how to approach the problem. For learning to occur, the student has to make decisions about the nature of the information and the steps needed to process the information.

ID has traditionally been seen as a deficiency in the area of learning. However, research shows that students with mild to moderate ID can, and do, learn academic and adaptive skills if appropriate learning strategies and explicit instructions are provided. The research presented in the guidelines provides stronger support for ID as a thinking disorder, rather than a learning disorder, since thinking appears to be a prerequisite for learning as well as part of the learning process.

The poorly developed social skills of students with ID are a major factor in drawing the attention of school and community personnel to their disability. One factor that restricts the self-determination and quality of life of individuals with ID is limited social and cognitive problem-solving skills. However, social problem-solving strategies can be learned and used when instructions are explicit.

Prevalence

According to the *Twenty-Sixth Annual Report* of the U.S. Department of Education (2004), 570,642 students between the ages of 6 and 21 were identified as having mental retardation. This represents approximately 10 percent of all students having a classification in special education, or about 2 percent of all school-age students.

The prevalence estimate of mental retardation varies in various research studies. The American Association on Mental Retardation estimates that 2.5 percent of the population has this disability (Luckasson, 2002).

Determining the Presence of Mental Retardation: Step by Step

Step I: Become Familiar With the Characteristics of Students With Mental Retardation

Students with mental retardation may

- Sit up, crawl, or walk later than other students
- Learn to talk later, or have trouble speaking
- Find it hard to remember things
- Not understand how to pay for things
- Have trouble understanding social rules
- Have trouble seeing the consequences of their actions
- Have trouble solving problems
- Have trouble thinking logically
- Exhibit failure to meet intellectual developmental markers
- Exhibit persistence of infantile behavior
- Lack curiosity
- Have decreased learning ability
- Have an inability to meet educational demands of school (National Library of Congress, 2005)

Individuals with mental retardation show a wide range of abilities, disabilities, strengths, and needs for support. It is common to find language delay and motor development significantly below the norms of peers who do not have mental retardation. More seriously affected students will experience delays in such areas of motor skills development as mobility, body image, and control of body actions. Compared to their peers without disabilities, students with mental retardation may generally be below norms in height and weight, may experience more speech problems, and may have a higher incidence of vision and hearing impairment.

In contrast to their classmates, students with mental retardation often have problems with attention, perception, memory, problem solving, and logical thought. They are slower in learning how to learn, and they find it harder to apply what they have learned to new situations or problems. Some professionals explain these patterns by asserting that students with mental retardation have qualitatively different deficits in cognition or memory. Others believe that persons with mental retardation move through the same stages of development as those without retardation, though at a slower rate, reaching lower levels of functioning overall.

Step II: Determine the Procedures and Assessment Measures

When a student has been referred for assessment to determine the presence of a disability, the IEP Committee reviews the documentation of the general education interventions used with the student. The team also collects and reviews a variety of readily available information about the student to determine whether additional formal information gathering is needed.

Examples of *sources of information* include, but are not limited to, the following:

- School records information from the teacher
- Classroom behavior
- Health record
- General education interventions
- Information from parent or guardian conferences or speech/ language interviews
- Discipline records
- Home behavior
- Hobbies and interests
- Neighborhood friendships

The following high-risk factors may indicate the presence of mental retardation:

- Academic skill development and adaptive behavior are below those of most, if not all, of the students in the class.
- Work samples evidence delay across all academic areas.
- Low performance level cannot be attributed to factors other than mental retardation (i.e., social/emotional, visual, or hearing problem).
- It is difficult for the student to retain information taught from one day to the next.
- There is a delay in development of gross and fine motor coordination.

The IEP Committee gathers all pertinent data (e.g., documentation of general education interventions, written records, observations, tests, and interviews) to identify the presence of factors indicative of mental retardation.

The assessment for the diagnosis of mental retardation needs to include

- An individual standardized intelligence test administered by a qualified professional
- An adaptive behavior scale
- A developmental history of the student
- A medical statement or a health assessment indicating whether any sensory or physical factors may be affecting the student's educational performance
- Assessments to determine the impact of the suspected disability

Step III: Determine the Eligibility for a Diagnosis of Mental Retardation

Based on the results of assessment, in order to meet eligibility standards for the diagnosis of mental retardation, a student has to meet all of the following requirements:

> **Important Point:** The eligibility criteria for classifications under IDEA are not specifically stated under the law. Therefore, the eligibility criteria for a particular disability may differ from state to state. The information pertaining to "eligibility" is the authors' professional interpretation based on reviewing the states' guidelines and criteria for mental retardation.

Determine Whether the Student Exhibits "Significantly Impaired Intellectual Functioning"

Significantly impaired intellectual functioning is two or more standard deviations below the mean, which usually indicates an IQ score of less than 70 when the standard deviation is 15.

Interpretation of evaluation results shall take into account factors that may affect test performance, including

- Limited English proficiency
- Cultural background and differences
- Medical conditions that impact school performance
- Socioeconomic status
- Communication, sensory, or motor disabilities

Difficulties in these areas cannot be the primary reason for significantly impaired scores on measures of intellectual functioning.

Determine Whether the Student Exhibits "Significantly Impaired Adaptive Behavior in the Home or Community"

Significantly impaired adaptive behavior can be determined by

- A composite score on an individual standardized instrument to be completed with or by the student's principal caretaker, which measures two standard deviations or more below the mean. Standard scores are used. A composite age equivalent score that represents a 50 percent delay based on chronological age can be used only if the instrument fails to provide a composite standard score. A composite score two or more standard deviations below the mean cannot be primarily the result of
  - Limited English proficiency
  - Cultural background and differences
  - Medical conditions that impact school performance
  - Socioeconomic status
  - Communication, sensory, or motor disabilities
- Additional documentation, which may be obtained from systematic documented observations, impressions, developmental history by an appropriate specialist in conjunction with the principal caretaker in the home, community, residential program, or institutional setting; and
- Significantly impaired adaptive behavior in the school, day care center, residence, or program as determined by
  - Systematic documented observations by an appropriate specialist, which compare the student with other students of his or her chronological age group. Observations should address age-appropriate adaptive behaviors. Adaptive behaviors to be observed in each age range are to include
    - o Birth–6 years—communication, self-care, social skills, and physical development
    - o 6–13 years—communication, self-care, social skills, home living, community use, self-direction, health and safety, functional academics, and leisure
    - o 14–21 years—communication, self-care, social skills, home living, community use, self-direction, health and safety, functional academics, leisure, and work
  - When appropriate, completion of an individual standardized instrument with the principal teacher of the student
  - Limited English proficiency
  - Cultural background and differences
  - Medical conditions that impact school performance

- Socioeconomic status
- Communication, sensory, or motor disabilities

Developmental History (Birth to Age 18) Indicates Delays in Cognitive/Intellectual Abilities and a Current Demonstration of Delays in Normal Development Present in the Student's Natural (Home and School) Environment

The Characteristics as Defined Above Can Cause an Adverse Effect on Educational Performance in the General Education Classroom or Learning Environment

Final Thoughts

Historically, mental retardation has either been described in controversial terms or presented as a clear-cut disability category. At various times, subcategories of mental retardation have been identified based on degree of severity, with concomitant labels such as "educable" versus "trainable," "moderate," "severe," and "profound." Recent systemic changes in education emphasize that "special education is a set of services brought to natural environments rather than a set of places where services are provided" (Iowa Department of Education, 1997). In such a system, all subcategories have disappeared.

Over the past decade, various groups (American Association on Mental Retardation, American Psychological Association) have attempted to shift the mental retardation model from one that is based on deficits in the individual to one based on levels of support needed by the individual with the disability. Efforts have also been made to substitute the label *intellectual disability* for *mental retardation* because the new label more accurately connotes the cognitive underpinning of the disability.

9

Multiple Disabilities

Definition Under IDEA

Under IDEA, the term *multiple disabilities* means *concomitant [simultane-ous] impairments (such as mental retardation-blindness, mental retardation-orthopedic impairment, etc.), the combination of which causes such severe educational needs that they cannot be accommodated in a special educa-tion program solely for one of the impairments. The term does not include deaf-blindness.* (34 C.F.R., sec. 300.7 (a)(c)(7))

Overview

According to Deutsch-Smith (2004, p. 448), people with multiple disabilities require ongoing and intensive supports across their school years and typically across their lives. For some, these supports may well be in only one life activity, but for many of these individuals, supports are needed for access and participation in mainstream society. Supports are necessary because most individuals with multi-ple disabilities require assistance in many adaptive areas.

No single definition covers all the conditions associated with severe and multiple disabilities. Schools usually link the two areas (severe dis-abilities and multiple disabilities) into a single category for students who have the most significant cognitive, physical, or communication impairments (Turnbull, Turnbull, & Wehmeyer, 2006, p. 232).

Prevalence

According to the *Twenty-Sixth Annual Report* of the U.S. Department of Education (2004), 131,225 students between the ages of 6 and 21 received special education services under the disability category of Multiple Disabilities. This makes up 2.2 percent of all school-age students receiving special education services.

Determining the Presence of Multiple Disabilities: Step by Step

Step I: Become Familiar With the Characteristics of Students With Multiple Disabilities

Individuals with severe or multiple disabilities may exhibit a wide range of characteristics, depending on the combination and severity of disabilities, and the person's age. They may share some traits, however, including

- Limited speech or communication
- Difficulty in basic physical mobility
- Tendency to forget skills through disuse
- Trouble generalizing skills from one situation to another
- A need for support in major life activities (e.g., domestic, leisure, community use, vocational; National Dissemination Center for Children with Disabilities, 2004d)

Multiple disabilities in an infant or a young student require the coordinated efforts of multiple experts (one from every identified disability area). Because of the interactive, multiplicative effects of multiple disabilities, it is essential that intervention and/or programming efforts be focused cooperatively on functional tasks. Whenever possible, intervention should be aimed toward minimizing or preventing DDs. Since there seems to be an ever-increasing number of infants and young students with multiple disabilities, the cooperative approach to early intervention seems to have the best potential for enhancing the potential of these students (Texas School for the Blind and Visually Impaired, 2003).

A variety of medical problems may accompany severe disabilities; examples include seizures, sensory loss, hydrocephalus, and scoliosis. These conditions should be considered when establishing school services (National Dissemination Center for Children with Disabilities, 2004d).

Step II: Determine the Procedures and Assessment Measures

A student with multiple disabilities is evaluated by the procedures for each disability and needs to meet the standards for two or more disabilities. If a student is suspected of having multiple disabilities, the following evaluation should be considered:

- An observation by a team member other than the student's general education teacher of the student's academic performance in a general classroom setting; or in the case of a student less than school age or out of school, an observation by a team member conducted in an age-appropriate environment
- A developmental history, if needed
- An assessment of intellectual ability
- Other assessments of the characteristics of speech and language impairments if the student exhibits impairments in any one or more of the following areas: cognition, fine motor, perceptual motor, communication, social or emotional, and perception or memory. These assessments are to be completed by specialists knowledgeable in the specific characteristics being assessed.
- A review of cumulative records, previous IEPs or IFSPs, and teacher-collected work samples
- If deemed necessary, a medical statement or health assessment statement indicating whether any physical factors may be affecting the student's educational performance
- Assessments to determine the impact of the suspected disability on the student's educational performance (ages kindergarten–21) or on the student's developmental progress (ages 3–kindergarten)
- Additional evaluations or assessments necessary to identify the student's educational needs

Step III: Determine the Eligibility for a Diagnosis of Multiple Disabilities

Important Point: The eligibility criteria for classifications under IDEA are not specifically stated under the law. Therefore, the eligibility criteria for a particular disability may differ from state to state. The information pertaining to "eligibility" is the authors' professional interpretation based on reviewing the states' guidelines and criteria for multiple disabilities.

To identify and be determined as eligible for special education services as a student with multiple disabilities, the IEP Committee documents that the following standards have been met:

The IEP Committee Must Determine That the Student Has the Following Two Characteristics

1. The student meets the standards for two or more identified disabilities.

2. The student is unable to benefit from services and supports designed for only one of the disabilities, as determined to be primary or secondary disabilities by the IEP Committee.

The IEP Committee Must Determine That

- The student has a combination of two or more disabilities
- The nature of the combination of disabilities requires significant developmental and educational programming that cannot be accommodated with special education services that primarily serve one area of the disability

The IEP Committee Must Determine That All Exclusionary Factors Have Been Ruled Out. An Individual Will Not Be Considered Eligible for Services Under Multiple Disabilities If One or More of the Following Exist

- The adverse effects are from a lack of instruction in reading or math that is not related to the traumatic brain injury.
- The adverse effects are from environmental, cultural, or economic disadvantage as a result of such factors as second language, limited English proficiency, other cultural values and experiences, and experiential differences.
- The adverse effects are judged to result from absenteeism (unrelated to health) or change in residence or schools.
- The disability is more accurately described by another category of eligibility.
- The student does not meet the eligibility criteria for deaf-blindness.

Final Thoughts

Early intervention programs, as well as preschool and educational programs with the appropriate support services, are important to students with sensory and additional disabilities (NEC Foundation of America, 2001).

At the present time, students with severe and multiple disabilities are taught in a variety of settings, from totally segregated to fully inclusive. The doctrine of the **least restrictive environment (LRE),** as applied to students with severe and multiple disabilities, has usually resulted in placement in a special education classroom within a general education school. Now an increasing number of leaders in the field of severe and multiple disabilities are advocating for full **inclusion** for these students. Successful collaboration is essential if students are to be fully included in schools and community settings. Because the students' needs can be extensive, families, educators, **physical** and **occupational therapists,** speech and language pathologists, and medical personnel need to work closely with each other to ensure that students receive an appropriate and inclusive education. In addition, students without disabilities and community members need to understand their roles in the collaborative planning process (Turnbull et al., 2004).

To effectively address the considerable needs of individuals with sensory and additional disabilities, educational programs need to incorporate a variety of components, including language and/or communication development, social skill development, functional skill development (i.e., self-help skills), and vocational skill development.

Related services are of great importance, and the appropriate therapists need to work closely with classroom teachers and parents or guardians. Best practices indicate that related services are best offered during the natural routine of the school and community rather than by removing the student from class for isolated therapy (Ohio Coalition for the Education of Children with Disabilities, 2005).

Classroom arrangements must take into consideration students' needs for medications, special diets, or special equipment. Adaptive aids and equipment enable students to increase their range of functioning. The use of computers, augmentative/alternative computer communication systems, communication boards, head sticks, and adaptive switches are some of the technological advances that enable students with sensory and additional disabilities to participate more fully in integrated settings.

Integration/inclusion with peers without disabilities is important for the development of social skills and friendships for students with sensory and additional disabilities.

These conditions should be considered when establishing school services. A multidisciplinary team consisting of the student's parents or guardians, educational specialists, and medical therapeutic specialists in the areas in which the individual demonstrates problems should work together to plan and coordinate necessary services (National Dissemination Center for Children with Disabilities, 2004d).

10

Orthopedic Impairment

Definition Under IDEA

A severe orthopedic impairment that adversely affects a student's educational performance. The term includes impairments due to the effects of congenital anomaly (e.g., clubfoot, absence of some member, etc.), impairments due to the effects of disease (e.g., poliomyelitis, bone tuberculosis, etc.), and impairments from other causes (e.g., cerebral palsy, amputations, and fractures or burns that cause contractures). (34 C.F.R. 300.7 (a)(c)(8))

Overview

Although IDEA uses the term *orthopedic impairments*, educators typically use the term *physical disabilities* when referring to these same conditions (Turnbull et al., 2006). A physical disability is a condition that interferes with a student's ability to use his or her body. Physical disabilities are conditions that affect movement, that is, an individual's motor control (e.g., walking, standing) and fine motor control (e.g., writing, holding, or manipulating small objects using the hands, oral motor skills; Friend, 2005).

Many, but not all, physical disabilities are orthopedic impairments (Kirk, Gallagher, & Anastasiow, 2000). According to Heward (2006,

p. 424), although IDEA uses the term *orthopedic impairments*, students with physical disabilities may have orthopedic impairments or neuromotor impairments. An orthopedic impairment involves the skeletal system—bones, joints, limbs, and associated muscles. A neuromotor impairment involves the central nervous system, affecting the ability to move, use, feel, or control certain parts of the body. Although orthopedic and neurological impairments are two distinct and separate types of disabilities, they may cause similar limitations in movement.

Students with orthopedic impairments, though few in number, comprise one of the most diverse group of **exceptional individuals** due to the many types of diseases and disorders that interfere with the normal functioning of the muscles or bones (Colarusso & O'Rourke, 2004). Individuals with physical disabilities often require highly specialized interventions to realize their maximum potential. Moreover, "the range of medical services, educational placements, and therapies is extremely diverse and highly specific to the person and his or her needs" (Hardman, Drew, & Egan, 2005, p. 473).

Prevalence

According to the *Twenty-Sixth Annual Report* of the U.S. Department of Education (2004), 74,000 students between the ages of 6 and 21 received special education services under the disability category of orthopedic impairments. This represents approximately 1.1 percent of all school-age students receiving special education services.

Determining the Presence of an Orthopedic Impairment: Step by Step

Step I: Become Familiar With the Characteristics of Students With Orthopedic Impairments

The characteristics of students with physical disabilities are so varied that attempting to describe them is nearly impossible (Heward, 2006). The reality is that it is difficult to generalize about such a broad spectrum of limitations (Bowe, 2005).

Orthopedic impairments are often divided into three main areas:

1. *Neuromotor impairments*—An abnormality of, or damage to, the brain, spinal cord, or nerves that send impulses to the muscles of the body (Gargiulo, 2004)

2. *Degenerative diseases*—Diseases that affect motor movement (Gargiulo, 2004)

3. *Musculoskelatal disorders*—Defects or diseases of the muscles or bones (Hallahan & Kauffman, 2006)

Step II: Determine the Procedures and Assessment Measures

If a student is suspected of having an orthopedic impairment, the following evaluation is conducted:

- A medical statement or a health assessment statement indicating a diagnosis of an orthopedic or a neuromotor impairment or a description of the motor impairment
- A standardized motor assessment, including the areas of fine motor, gross motor, and self-help, when appropriate, by a specialist knowledgeable about orthopedic or neuromotor development
- Assessments to determine the impact of the suspected disability on the student's educational performance (ages kindergarten–21) or on the student's development progress (ages 3–kindergarten)
- Additional evaluations or assessments necessary to identify the student's educational needs

If a student is suspected of having an orthopedic impairment under the definition set forth in IDEA, the following assessment measures should also be considered:

- An observation by a team member other than the student's general education teacher of the student's academic performance in a general classroom setting; or in the case of a student less than school age or out of school, an observation by a team member conducted in an age-appropriate environment
- A developmental history, if needed
- An assessment of intellectual ability
- Other assessments of the characteristics of speech and language impairments if the student exhibits impairments in any one or more of the following areas: cognition, fine motor, perceptual motor, communication, social or emotional, and perception or memory. These assessments are completed by specialists knowledgeable in the specific characteristics being assessed.

- A review of cumulative records, previous IEPs or IFSPs, and teacher-collected work samples
- If deemed necessary, a medical statement or health assessment statement indicating whether any physical factors may be affecting the student's educational performance
- Assessments to determine the impact of the suspected disability on the student's educational performance (ages kindergarten–21) or on the student's developmental progress (ages 3–kindergarten)
- Additional evaluations or assessments necessary to identify the student's educational needs

Step III: Determine the Eligibility for a Diagnosis of an Orthopedic Impairment

Important Point: The eligibility criteria for classifications under IDEA are not specifically stated under the law. Therefore, the eligibility criteria for a particular disability may differ from state to state. The information pertaining to "eligibility" is the authors' professional interpretation based on reviewing the states' guidelines and criteria for orthopedic impairments.

In general, states use two different methods to determine whether a student meets the eligibility criteria as a student with an orthopedic impairment under IDEA. We present a synopsis of these two options for an IEP Committee to consider.

Option 1

A student suspected of having an orthopedic impairment is eligible and in need of special education instruction and services if he or she meets the criterion in item a and one of the criteria in item b:

a. There must be documentation of a medically diagnosed physical impairment.

b. • The student's need for special education instruction and service is supported by a lack of functional level in organizational or independent work skills as verified by a minimum of two or more documented, systematic observations in daily routine settings, one of which is completed by a physical and health disabilities teacher.
   • The student's need for special education instruction and service is supported by an inability to manage or complete motoric portions of classroom tasks within time constraints as verified by a minimum of two or more documented

systematic observations in daily routine settings, one of which is completed by a physical and health disabilities teacher.

- The student's physical impairment interferes with educational performance as shown by an achievement deficit of 1.0 standard deviation or more below the mean on an individually administered, nationally normed standardized evaluation of the student's academic achievement.

Option 2

One condition from each of the following criteria must be judged to have been met in order for the student to be eligible for the category Orthopedic Impairment:

- *Physical Criteria for Eligibility*—The student has a diagnosis from a medical doctor of one or more of the following orthopedic conditions, which are temporary or permanent and may require adaptations in the physical plant: (1) impairments caused by congenital anomaly (e.g., clubfoot, absence of some member); (2) impairments caused by disease (e.g., poliomyelitis, bone tuberculosis); (3) impairments from other causes (e.g., cerebral palsy, amputations, and fractures or burns that cause contractures).
- *Academic Criteria for Eligibility*—An assessment of motor function in the educational environment (conducted by the physical and/or occupational therapist) must demonstrate the following adverse affects on educational performance that requires specialized instruction because of (1) a lack of meaningful and productive participation, (2) reduced efficiency in school work, (3) inability to access educational environment despite environmental modifications.

Exclusionary Factors

An individual will not be considered eligible for services under Orthopedic Impairment if one or more of the following exist:

- The adverse effect is from a lack of instruction in reading or math that is not related to the health impairment.
- The adverse effect is from environmental, cultural, or economic disadvantage as a result of such factors as second language, limited English proficiency, other cultural values and experiences, and experiential differences.

- The adverse effect is judged to result from absenteeism (unre-lated to health) or change in residence or schools.
- The disability is more accurately described by another category of eligibility.
- The adverse effect is primarily due to active substance abuse.

Final Thoughts

A critical educational consideration for students with orthopedic impairments is placement. Educational services for these students may be provided in a variety of settings depending on the type and severity of the condition, the services available in the community, and the medical prognosis for the condition (Hallahan & Kauffman, 2006). Educational placement options include general education classrooms, **resource rooms,** special classes, and other, more restrictive settings (e.g., special classrooms, special schools, residential facilities, and/or hospital and **homebound** programs).

Most students with orthopedic/physical impairments spend at least part of the day in general classrooms (Bowe, 2005). According to the U.S. Department of Education (2004), approximately 46 percent of all school-age students who received special education services under the disability category of Orthopedic Impairment were educated in general classrooms. Twenty-three percent received resource room services. Finally, almost one third received their education in a special classroom or more restrictive environment (U.S. Department of Education, 2004).

It is often necessary to modify and adapt the school environment to make it accessible, safe, and less restrictive. Accessibility guidelines are readily available, and when these guidelines are followed the environment becomes easier for the student to manage independently. Environmental modifications include instituting adaptations to provide increased access to a task or an activity, changing the way instruction is delivered, and modifying how the task is done (Best, Heller, & Bigge, 2005; Heller, Dangel, & Sweatman, 1995; Heward, 2006).

In conclusion, it is impossible to specify the content of the educational curriculum for learners with physical disabilities because there is so much variation with regard to need. Some students will need only minor modifications, whereas others with more severe disabilities will require extensive adaptations. However, it should be emphasized that teachers will need to work closely with professionals from other disciplines to meet the needs of these learners. In most cases, educating students with physical disabilities is not so much a matter of special instruction for students with disabilities as it is of educating the nondisabled population (Closs, 2000).

11

Other Health Impairments

Definition Under IDEA

Having limited strength, vitality or alertness, including a heightened alertness to environmental stimuli, that results in limited alertness with respect to the educational environment, that is due to chronic or acute health problems such as asthma, attention deficit disorder or attention deficit hyperactivity disorder, diabetes, epilepsy, a heart condition, hemophilia, lead poisoning, leukemia, nephritis, rheumatic fever, and sickle cell anemia; and adversely affects a student's educational performance. (34 C.F.R. 300.7 (a)(c)(9))

Overview

Many conditions and diseases can significantly affect a student's health and ability to function successfully in school. Most health impairments are chronic conditions; that is, they are always present, or they recur. By contrast, an acute condition develops quickly with intense symptoms that last a relatively short period of time. To be served under the Other Health Impairments (OHI) category, the student's health condition must limit strength, vitality, or alertness to such a degree that the student's educational progress is adversely affected. More than 200 specific health impairments exist, and most are rare (Turnbull et al., 2006; cited in Pierangelo & Giuliani, in press).

Within the category of OHI is ADHD. Only time will tell whether ADHD finds its way to another special education category or whether it becomes a category of its own in the future. Presently, the inclusion of ADHD has caused a significant increase in the size of the category (U.S. Department of Education, 2001).

Prevalence

According to the *Twenty-Sixth Annual Report* of the U.S. Department of Education (2004), 449,093 students between the ages of 6 and 21 were identified as having OHI. This represents approximately 7.5 percent of all students having a classification in special education, or less than 1 percent of all school-age students.

Determining the Presence of an Other Health Impairment: Step by Step

Step I: Become Familiar With the Characteristics of Students With Other Health Impairments

According to the Starbright Foundation (2002; cited in Turnbull et al., 2004), students with health impairments face numerous complex challenges. Common issues are "loss of sense of control, lack of understanding about the condition, fear, worry, anxiety, stress, anger, and guilt, changes in family dynamics, isolation, medical noncompliance, boredom, depression, pain, decreased self-esteem, negative body image, and impact on identity and social interactions, including those at school" (p. 313).

Some general characteristics faced by individuals with OHI may include but are not limited to

- Fatigue
- Mobility issues
- Issues involving attention
- Coordination difficulties

- Muscle weakness
- Frequent absences or lateness to school
- Stamina
- Inability to concentrate for long periods of time

Step II: Determine the Procedures and Assessment Measures

If a student is suspected of having an OHI, the following evaluation is conducted:

- A medical statement or a health assessment statement, indicating a diagnosis of a health impairment or a description of the impairment, and a statement that the student's condition is permanent or is expected to last more than 60 calendar days
- Assessments to determine the impact of the suspected disability on the student's educational performance (ages kindergarten–21) or on the student's developmental progress (ages 3–kindergarten)
- Additional evaluations or assessments necessary to identify the student's educational needs. If a student is suspected of having a health impairment under the definition set forth in IDEA, the following assessment measures should also be considered:
  - An observation by a team member other than the student's general education teacher of the student's academic performance in a general classroom setting; or in the case of a student less than school age or out of school, an observation by a team member conducted in an age-appropriate environment
  - A developmental history, if needed
  - An assessment of intellectual ability
  - Other assessments of the characteristics of speech and language impairments if the student exhibits impairments in any one or more of the following areas: cognition, fine motor, perceptual motor, communication, social or emotional, and perception or memory. These assessments are made by specialists knowledgeable in the specific characteristics being assessed.
  - A review of cumulative records, previous IEPs or IFSPs, and teacher-collected work samples

Step III: Determine the Eligibility for a Diagnosis of an Other Health Impairment

To identify and be considered eligible for special education services as a student with an orthopedic impairment, the IEP Committee documents that the following standards have been met:

- The IEP Committee has obtained a medical statement or a health assessment statement indicating a diagnosis of health impairment or a description of the impairment, and showing that the student's condition is permanent or is expected to last more than 60 days.
- The student exhibits limited strength, vitality, or alertness, including a heightened alertness to environmental stimuli that results in limited alertness with respect to the educational environment.
- The student's limited strength, vitality, or alertness is due to a chronic or acute health problem.
- The student's condition is permanent or is expected to last more than 60 calendar days.
- The student's disability has an adverse impact on the student's educational performance (ages kindergarten–21) or on the student's developmental progress (ages 3–kindergarten).
- The student needs special education services.

Final Thoughts

When responsible educators encounter diseases and conditions they know little about, they seek out all the information they need to provide an appropriate education to students involved (Deutsch-Smith, 2004). One of the main considerations in the education of these students is the use of the team approach in developing and carrying out a student's educational program. The team generally includes the parents or guardians, teachers, medical professionals, and health-related professionals such as a physical therapist.

Parents or guardians are critical members of the team and should be involved in all educational decisions. Sirvis (1988) noted that the team should design a program that meets the needs of the student in five basic goal areas: "(a) physical independence, including mastery of daily living skills; (b) self-awareness and social maturation; (c) communication; (d) academic growth; and (e) life skills training" (p. 400). Interdisciplinary services such as occupational and physical therapy and speech and language therapy are of prime importance for youngsters who have physical disabilities.

It is often necessary to modify and adapt the school environment to make it accessible, safe, and less restrictive since discriminating architecture does not have to discriminate (Leibrock & Terry, 1999, p. 17). Accessibility guidelines are readily available, and when these guidelines are followed the environment becomes easier for the student to manage independently.

Finally, what role teachers should play in the medical management of students is an ongoing and contentious issue (Temple, 2000) since teachers are being called on to assume more responsibilities for the medical management of their students (Heller, Frederic, Best, Dykes, & Cohen, 2000).

12

Speech and Language Impairments (Communication Disorders)

Definition Under IDEA

> A speech or language impairment is defined as *a communication disorder, such as stuttering, impaired articulation, language impairment, or a voice impairment that adversely affects a student's educational performance.* (34 C.F.R. 300.7 (a)(c)(11))

Overview

Students with communication disorders have deficits in their ability to exchange information with others. A communication disorder may occur in the realm of language, speech, and/or hearing. Language difficulties include spoken language, reading, and/or writing difficulties. Speech encompasses such areas as articulation and phonology (the ability to speak clearly and be intelligible), fluency (stuttering), and voice. Hearing difficulties may also encompass speech problems (e.g., articulation or voice) and/or language problems. Hearing impairments include deafness and hearing loss, which, as noted earlier, can result from a conductive loss, a sensorineural loss, a mixed loss, or a central hearing loss.

Communication disorders may result from many different conditions. For example, language-based learning disabilities are the result of a difference in brain structure present at birth. This particular difficulty may be genetically based. Other communication disorders stem from oral-motor difficulties (e.g., an apraxia or dysarthia of speech), aphasias (difficulties resulting from a stroke, which may involve motor, speech, and/or language problems), traumatic brain injuries, and stuttering, which is now believed to be a neurological deficit. The most common conditions that affect students' communication include language-based learning disabilities, attention deficit disorder, ADHD, cerebral palsy, **mental disabilities,** cleft lip or palate, and ASD.

The functions, skills, and abilities of voice, speech, and language are related. Some dictionaries and textbooks use the terms almost interchangeably, but for scientists and medical professionals, it is important to distinguish among them.

Voice

Voice (or vocalization) is the sound produced by humans and other vertebrates using the lungs and the vocal folds in the larynx, or voice box. Voice is not always produced as speech, however. Infants babble and coo; animals bark, moo, whinny, growl, and meow; and adult humans laugh, sing, and cry. Voice is generated by airflow from the lungs as the vocal folds are brought close together. When air is pushed past the vocal folds with sufficient pressure, the vocal folds vibrate. If the vocal folds in the larynx did not vibrate normally, speech could only be produced as a whisper. Your voice is as unique as your fingerprint. It helps define your personality, mood, and health.

Approximately 7.5 million people in the United States have trouble using their voices. Disorders of the voice involve problems with pitch, loudness, and quality. Pitch is the highness or lowness of a sound based on the frequency of the sound waves. Loudness is the perceived volume (or amplitude) of the sound, while quality refers to the character or distinctive attributes of a sound. Many people who have normal speaking skills have great difficulty communicating when their vocal apparatus fails. This can occur if the nerves controlling the larynx are impaired because of an accident, a surgical procedure, a viral infection, or cancer.

Speech

Humans express thoughts, feelings, and ideas *orally* to one another through a series of complex movements that alter and mold the basic tone created by voice into specific, decodable sounds. Speech is produced by precisely coordinated muscle actions in the head, neck, chest, and abdomen. Speech development is a gradual process that requires years of practice. During this process, a student learns how to regulate these muscles to produce understandable speech.

By the first grade, however, roughly 5 percent of students have noticeable speech disorders; the majority of these speech disorders have no known cause. One category of speech disorder is fluency disorder, or stuttering, which is characterized by a disruption in the flow of speech. It includes repetitions of speech sounds, hesitations before and during speaking, and the prolonged emphasis of speech sounds. More than 15 million individuals in the world stutter, most of whom began stuttering at a very early age. The majority of speech sound disorders in the preschool years occur in students who are developing normally in all other areas. Speech disorders also may occur in students who have developmental disabilities.

Language

Language is the expression of human communication through which knowledge, belief, and behavior can be experienced, explained, and shared. This sharing is based on systematic, conventionally used signs, sounds, gestures, or marks that convey understood meanings within a group or community. Recent research identifies "windows of opportunity" for acquiring language—written, spoken, or signed—that exist within the first few years of life.

Prevalence

According to the *Twenty-Sixth Annual Report* of the U.S. Department of Education (2004), 1,118,543 students between the ages of 6 and 21 were identified as having speech and language impairments. This represents approximately 19 percent of all students who have a classification in special education, or about 1.7 percent of all school-age students (Hunt & Marshall, 2005). This estimate does not include students who have speech/language problems secondary to other conditions such as mental retardation, traumatic brain injury, autism, cerebral palsy, and deafness (Friend, 2005).

Determining the Presence of a Speech and Language Impairment: Step by Step

Step I: Become Familiar With the Characteristics of Students With Speech and Language Impairments

A student with a communication problem may present many different symptoms, including difficulty following directions, attending to a conversation, pronouncing words, perceiving what was said, expressing oneself, or being understood because of a stutter or a hoarse voice. A student's communication is considered delayed when the student is noticeably behind his or her peers in the acquisition of speech and/or language skills. Sometimes a student will have greater receptive (understanding) than expressive (speaking) language skills, but this is not always the case.

Speech disorders refer to difficulties producing speech sounds or problems with voice quality. They might be characterized by an interruption in the flow or rhythm of speech, such as stuttering, which is called dysfluency. Speech disorders may be problems with the way sounds are formed, called articulation or phonological disorders, or they may be difficulties with the pitch, volume, or quality of the voice. Or a combination of several problems may be present. People with speech disorders have trouble using some speech sounds, which can also be a symptom of a delay. They may say "see" when they mean "ski," or they may have trouble using other sounds like "l" or "r." Listeners may have trouble understanding what someone with a speech disorder is trying to say. People with voice disorders may have trouble with the way their voices sound.

A language disorder is an impairment in the ability to understand and/or use words in context, both verbally and nonverbally. Some characteristics of language disorders include improper use of words and their meanings, inability to express ideas, inappropriate grammatical patterns, reduced vocabulary, and inability to follow directions. One or a combination of these characteristics may occur in students who are affected by language learning disabilities or developmental language delay. Students may hear or see a word but not be able to understand its meaning. They may have trouble getting others to understand what they are trying to communicate.

Problems with language may involve difficulty expressing ideas coherently, learning new vocabulary, understanding questions, following directions, recalling information, understanding and remembering something that has just been said, reading at a satisfactory pace, comprehending spoken or read material, learning the alphabet, identifying sounds that correspond to letters, perceiving the correct order of letters in words, and, possibly, spelling. Difficulties with speech may include being unintelligible owing to a motor problem or to poor learning. Sounding hoarse, breathy, or harsh may be due to a voice problem. Stuttering also affects speech intelligibility because it interrupts the student's flow of speech.

Step II: Determine the Procedures and Assessment Measures

Speech/language impairments are determined through the demonstration of impairments in the areas of language, articulation, voice, and fluency:

- *Language Impairment.* A significant deficiency that is not consistent with the student's chronological age in one or more of the following areas:
  - A deficiency in receptive language skills to gain information
  - A deficiency in expressive language skills to communicate information
  - A deficiency in processing (auditory perception) skills to organize information
- *Articulation Impairment.* A significant deficiency in ability to produce sounds in conversational speech, which is not consistent with chronological age.
- *Voice Impairment.* An excess or significant deficiency in pitch, intensity, or quality resulting from pathological conditions or inappropriate use of the vocal mechanism.
- *Fluency Impairment.* An abnormal interruption in the flow of speech by repetitions or prolongations of a sound or syllable or by avoidance and struggle behaviors.

Language Impairment

If a student is suspected of having a speech and language impairment, the following procedures and assessment measures should be used: For a language impairment, a significant deficiency in language is determined by a minimum of two measures, including criterion- and/or norm-referenced instruments, functional communication analyses, and language samples. At least one standardized comprehensive measure of language ability should be included in the evaluation process.

Evaluation of language abilities includes the following:

- Hearing screening
- Reception: vocabulary, syntax, morphology
- Expression: mean length of utterance, syntax, semantics, pragmatics, morphology
- Auditory perception: selective attention, discrimination, memory, sequencing, association, and integration
- Documentation and assessment of how a language impairment adversely affects educational performance in the classroom or learning environment

Articulation Impairment

A significant deficiency in articulation is determined by evaluation of articulation abilities including the following:

- Appropriate formal/informal instrument(s)
- Stimulability probes
- Oral peripheral examination
- Analysis of phoneme production in conversational speech
- Documentation and assessment of how an articulation impairment adversely affects educational performance in the general education classroom or learning environment

Voice Impairment

Evaluation of vocal characteristics includes the following:

- Hearing screening
- Examination by an otolaryngologist
- Oral peripheral examination
- Documentation and assessment of how a voice impairment adversely affects educational performance in the general education classroom or learning environment

Fluency Impairment

Evaluation of fluency includes the following:

- Hearing screening
- Information obtained from parents or guardians, students, and teacher(s) regarding nonfluent behaviors/attitudes across communication situations
- Oral peripheral examination
- Documentation and assessment of how a fluency impairment adversely affects educational performance in the general education classroom or learning environment

If a student is suspected of having a speech and language impairment under the definition set forth in IDEA, the following additional assessment measures should also be considered:

- An observation by a team member other than the student's general education teacher of the student's academic performance in a general classroom setting; or in the case of a student less than school age or out of school, an observation by a team member conducted in an age-appropriate environment
- A developmental history, if needed
- An assessment of intellectual ability
- Other assessments of the characteristics of speech and language impairments if the student exhibits impairments in any one or more of the following areas: cognition, fine motor, perceptual motor, communication, social or emotional, and perception or memory. These assessments are to be completed by specialists knowledgeable in the specific characteristics being assessed.
- A review of cumulative records, previous IEPs or IFSPs, and teacher-collected work samples
- If deemed necessary, a medical statement or health assessment statement indicating whether any physical factors may be affecting the student's educational performance
- Assessments to determine the impact of the suspected disability on the student's educational performance (ages kindergarten–21) or on the student's developmental progress (ages 3–kindergarten)
- Additional evaluations or assessments necessary to identify the student's educational needs

Step III: Determine the Eligibility for a Diagnosis of a Speech and Language Impairment

Important Point: The eligibility criteria for classifications under IDEA are not specifically stated under the law. Therefore, the eligibility criteria for a particular disability may differ from state to state. The information pertaining to "eligibility" is the authors' professional interpretation based on reviewing the states' guidelines and criteria for speech and language impairment.

Four types of speech or language impairments are generally recognized:

1. *Fluency disorder*: the intrusion or repetition of sounds, syllables, and words; prolongation of sounds; avoidance of words; silent blocks; or inappropriate inhalation, exhalation, or phonation patterns. These patterns may also be accompanied by facial and body movements associated with the effort to speak.

2. *Voice disorder*: the absence of voice or the presence of abnormal quality, pitch, resonance, loudness, or duration

3. *Articulation disorder*: the absence of or incorrect production of speech sounds or phonological processes that are developmentally appropriate (e.g., lisp, difficulty articulating certain sounds, such as l or r)

4. *Language disorder*: a breakdown in communication as characterized by problems in expressing needs, ideas, or information that may be accompanied by problems in understanding

Many states identify students with one of these four types of speech and language impairments using two methods.

Determination of Eligibility: Method 1

To identify and be considered eligible for special education services as a student with a speech and language impairment, the IEP Committee documents that the following standards have been met. Based on the results of the assessment:

- Determine that the student meets one or more of the following criteria (a–d):
  a. For a voice impairment, determine whether (i) the student demonstrates chronic vocal characteristics that deviate in at least one of the areas of pitch, quality, intensity, or resonance; (ii) the student's voice disorder impairs communication or

intelligibility; (iii) the student's voice disorder is rated as moderate to severe on a voice assessment scale.

b. For a fluency impairment, determine whether (i) the student demonstrates an interruption in the rhythm or rate of speech that is characterized by hesitations, repetitions, or prolongation of sounds, syllables, words, or phrases; (ii) the student's fluency disorder interferes with communication and calls attention to itself across two or more settings; (iii) the student demonstrates moderate to severe vocal dysfluencies, or the student evidences associated secondary behaviors such as struggling or avoidance, as measured by a standardized measure.

c. For a phonological or articulation impairment, determine whether (i) the student's phonology or articulation is rated significantly discrepant as measured by a standardized test; (ii) the disorder is substantiated by a language sample or other evaluation(s).

d. For a syntax, morphology, pragmatic, or semantic impairment, determine whether (i) the student's language in the area of syntax, morphology, pragmatics, or semantics is significantly discrepant as measured by standardized test(s); (ii) the disorder is substantiated by a language sample or other evaluation(s); (iii) the disorder is not the result of another disability.

- Determine whether the student's disability has an adverse impact on educational performance. The student's disability must have an adverse impact on educational performance (ages kindergarten–21) or on the student's developmental progress (ages 3–kindergarten).
- Determine that the eligibility is not due to a lack of instruction in reading or math, or due to limited English proficiency.
- Determine whether the student needs special education services.

Determination of Eligibility: Method 2

A speech or language impairment is demonstrated by significant deficits in listening comprehension or oral expression. The IEP Committee obtains an opinion from a licensed speech-language pathologist as to the existence of a speech or language impairment and its effect on the student's ability to function. A speech or language impairment is determined on the basis of the following criteria:

- Determine whether a deficit exists in listening comprehension. A significant deficit in listening comprehension exists when a

student demonstrates a significant deficit from the test mean on one or more measures of auditory processing or comprehension of connected speech. Auditory processing or comprehension includes
- Semantics
- Syntax
- Phonology
- Recall of information
- Following directions
- Pragmatics
- Determine whether a deficit exists in oral expression. For purposes of determining a speech and language impairment, a significant deficit in oral expression exists when a student demonstrates one or more of the following conditions:
  - *Voice.* A significant deficit in voice exists when both of the following are present: (i) documentation by an otolaryngologist that treatment is indicated for a vocal pathology or speech-related medical condition, and (ii) abnormal vocal characteristics in pitch, quality, nasality, volume, or breath support, which persist for at least one month.
  - *Fluency.* A significant deficit in fluency exists when the student exhibits one or more of the following behaviors:
    o Part word repetitions or sound prolongations occurring on at least 5 percent of the words spoken in two or more speech samples
    o Sound or silent prolongations exceeding one second in two or more speech samples
    o Secondary symptoms or signs of tension or struggle during speech, which are so severe as to interfere with the flow of communication
  - *Articulation.* A significant deficit in articulation attributed to an organic or functional disorder exists when a student is unable to articulate two or more of the unrelated phonemes in connected speech, and it is not attributed to dialect or second-language difficulties.
  - *Oral Discourse.* A significant deficit exists when a student demonstrates a deficit of at least two standard deviations from the test mean on one or more measures of oral discourse. Oral discourse includes
    o Syntax
    o Semantics
    o Phonology
    o Pragmatics

- Determine whether the student's disability has an adverse impact on educational performance. The student's disability must have an adverse impact on educational performance (ages kindergarten–21) or on the student's developmental progress (ages 3–kindergarten).
- Determine that the eligibility is not due to a lack of instruction in reading or math, or due to limited English proficiency.
- Determine whether the student needs special education services.

Final Thoughts

The IEP Committee may not identify a student who exhibits any of the following as having a speech or language impairment:

- Mild, transitory, or developmentally appropriate speech or language difficulties that students experience at various times and to various degrees
- Speech or language performance that is consistent with developmental levels as documented by formal and informal assessment data unless the student requires speech or language services in order to benefit from his or her educational programs in school, home, and community environments
- Speech or language difficulties resulting from dialectical differences or from learning English as a second language, unless the student has a language impairment in his or her native language
- Difficulties with auditory processing without a concomitant documented oral speech or language impairment
- A tongue thrust that exists in the absence of a concomitant impairment in speech sound production
- Elective or selective mutism or school phobia without a documented oral speech or language impairment

Finally, a strong relationship exists between communication and academic achievement. Language and communication proficiency, along with academic success, depend on whether students can match their communications to the learning-teaching style of the classroom. Students with communication disorders are capable of high academic success if they learn the classroom's social, language, and learning patterns. Teachers and speech-language pathologists should focus their attention on classroom interactions and on the language and communications used within the school in order to help students learn to communicate in these environments. Explicit language and communication planning as well as nondeliberate language use (e.g., unconscious choice of language) are important features of the school and class environments that provide opportunities for teaching and learning.

13

Traumatic Brain Injury

Definition Under IDEA

IDEA defines traumatic brain injury (TBI) as *an acquired injury to the brain caused by an external physical force, resulting in total or partial functional disability or psychosocial impairment, or both, that adversely affects a student's educational performance. The term applies to open or closed head injuries resulting in impairments in one or more areas, such as cognition; language; memory; attention; reasoning; abstract thinking; judgment; problem-solving; sensory, perceptual, and motor abilities; psychosocial behavior; physical functions; information processing; and speech. The term does not apply to brain injuries that are congenital or degenerative, or to brain injuries induced by birth trauma.* (34 C.F.R. 300.7 (a)(c)(12))

Overview

The frequency of TBI in students is staggering. Each year in the United States as many as one million students and youth will sustain TBIs from motor vehicle accidents, falls, sports, and abuse. The largest group of traumatic brain injured individuals fall within the 15–24 age group, but the frequency is nearly as high for students and youth under 15 years of age.

TBI, also referred to as acquired brain injury or ABI (Brain Injury Association of America, 2004), is sudden physical damage to the brain. The damage may be due to the effects of the head forcefully hitting an object such as the dashboard of a car (closed head injury) or due to something passing through the skull and piercing the brain (penetrating head injury or open head injury), as in a gunshot wound (Michaud, Semel-Concepcion, Duhaime, & Lazar, 2002).

While young students may physically recover more quickly from serious accidents than adults, the long-term cognitive and/or behavioral problems are often more pronounced. Generally speaking, the younger the student, the more profound the long-term effects will be. Injury to a developing brain alters the ongoing development. Although previously learned information is often retained, new learning may be difficult. Younger students do not have the same knowledge base to build upon and may experience greater difficulty mastering new skills.

Because childhood injuries occur when brains are still developing, some deficits may not be apparent to the parent or guardian until later in life when those developmental skills are required. It is recommended that both documentation of the brain injury and monitoring over time for delayed consequences be addressed.

The term *TBI* is not used for a person who is born with a brain injury. Nor is it used for brain injuries that happen during birth. The term is reserved for head injuries that can cause changes in one or more areas, such as thinking and reasoning, understanding words, remembering things, paying attention, solving problems, thinking abstractly, talking, behaving, walking and other physical activities, seeing and/or hearing, and learning (Hallahan & Kauffman, 2006).

Prevalence

According to the *Twenty-Sixth Annual Report* of the U.S. Department of Education (2004), during the 2003–2004 school year, 22,459 students ages 6 to 21 (or 0.4 percent of all students with disabilities) received special education services under the IDEA category of Traumatic Brain Injury.

TBI is the most common cause of disability and death in the United States. More than one million students receive brain injuries each year (Keyser-Marcus et al., 2002). More than 30,000 of these students have lifelong disabilities as a result of the brain injury.

Annual statistics dramatically tell the story of head injury in the United States:

- Approximately 270,000 people experience a moderate or severe TBI.
- Approximately 70,000 people die from head injury.
- Approximately 1 million head-injured people are treated in hospital emergency rooms.
- Approximately 60,000 new cases of epilepsy occur as a result of head trauma.
- Approximately 230,000 people are hospitalized for TBI and survive (National Dissemination Center for Children with Disabilities, 2004e).

Determining the Presence of a Traumatic Brain Injury: Step by Step

Step I: Become Familiar With the Characteristics of Students With Traumatic Brain Injuries

The physical, behavioral, or mental changes that may result from head trauma depend on the areas of the brain that are injured. Nearly any domain of functioning can be affected by TBI (Clark, Russman, & Orme, 1999; Keyser-Marcus et al., 2002).

Most injuries cause focal brain damage, that is, damage confined to a small area in the brain. The focal damage is most often at the point where the head hits an object or where an object, such as a bullet, enters the brain.

In addition to focal damage, closed head injuries frequently cause diffuse brain injuries or damage to several other areas of the brain. The diffuse damage occurs when the impact of the injury causes the brain to move back and forth against the inside of the bony skull. The frontal and temporal lobes of the brain, the major speech and language areas, often receive the most damage in this way because they sit in pockets of the skull that allow more room for the brain to shift and sustain injury. Because these major speech and language areas often receive damage, communication difficulties frequently occur following closed head injuries. Other problems may include voice, swallowing, walking, balance, and coordination difficulties, as well as changes in the ability to smell and in memory and cognitive (or thinking) skills (Minnesota Department of Education, 2004).

According to Hallahan and Kauffman (2006, p. 433), the possible effects of TBI include a long list of learning and psychosocial problems, such as the following:

- Problems remembering things
- Problems learning new information
- Speech and/or language problems
- Difficulty sequencing things
- Difficulty in processing information
- Extremely uneven progress
- Inappropriate manners or mannerisms
- Failure to understand humor or social situations
- Becoming easily tired, frustrated, or angered
- Unreasonable fear or anxiety
- Irritability
- Sudden, exaggerated swings of mood
- Depression
- Aggression
- Perseveration

Generally speaking, TBIs in students are often diffuse and can affect many areas and functions within the brain. Since areas of the brain are interconnected, damage to any part of the system can often result in cognitive, motor, sensory, emotional, and behavioral changes. Frontal and temporal lobe damage can often occur in a TBI and may result in possible changes in personality and behavior, as well as deficits in memory, judgment, reasoning, problem solving, and inhibition. Difficulties with perceptual skills and expressive language may also result. When damage occurs in additional parts of the brain, changes may take place in motor or sensory functioning (Minnesota Department of Education, 2004).

Step II: Determine the Procedures and Assessment Measures

Special education evaluation of students with TBI poses many challenges. Results will affect eligibility for services and educational programming. To be considered, the student must have a documented medical diagnosis of TBI before a special education evaluation is initiated. The evaluation is then conducted to determine the existence of educational needs related to the brain injury. If a student has been recently evaluated in a clinical or medical setting as a result of a TBI, this information should be considered and incorporated into the school evaluation.

The special education evaluation team should include a special education professional who is knowledgeable and has training in the area of TBI. In addition to the parents or guardians, other team members may include a licensed special education teacher, school nurse, school psychologist, **adaptive physical education** teacher, general education teacher, and other appropriate related service providers.

Traditional psychometric tests may provide useful information, but must be used with caution because test scores may not reflect the student's educational needs and/or dysfunctions displayed in the classroom. The student's ability to carry out day-to-day tasks in the classroom and educational environment should be the primary focus of the evaluation.

Many teams also choose to conduct a functional academic evaluation, which includes interviews and observations in the areas of organization, study skills, work completion, and interaction/functional communication skills.

Since recovery from TBI can be sporadic and unpredictable, periodic reevaluation is important in order to monitor progress, review instructional objectives, and revise programs. Rapid changes in many areas of the student's functioning during the first year after injury may require more frequent evaluations to avoid basing intervention strategies and accommodations on outdated information. However, overtesting can also result in frustration for the student without significant results. The team must carefully consider decisions regarding type and frequency of evaluations.

The following nine domains of evaluation should be addressed to determine a functional impairment in one or more areas. Listed under each area are some indicators of functional impairments that may result from a TBI.

1. Intellectual/Cognitive Functioning Indicators

- **Distractibility,** poor concentration, and poor impulse control (disinhibition)
- Poor memory affecting encoding, retention, and retrieval of information
- Visual-spatial problems affecting part–whole reasoning, integration, and synthesis
- Impaired judgment, conceptual reasoning, and organizational skills

- Slow processing speed and slow output of information affecting performance timed tests

2. Academic Performance Indicators

- Impaired word recognition (dyslexia) or reading comprehension
- Confusion with math calculations, especially applications (**dyscalculia**)
- Poor retention of facts in content subjects, such as history and science
- Errors in mechanics and fluent expression of written language (**dysgraphia**)
- Difficulty integrating and applying new information

3. Communicative Status Indicators

- Oral motor dysfunction affecting articulation or swallowing
- Comprehension problems or inefficiently processing language
- Dysfluent speech or problems retrieving words from memory
- Pragmatic language deficits in conversation, turn-taking, and social rules

4. Motor Ability Indicators

Gross Motor
- Extreme weakness (paresis) or total paralysis of one or both sides
- Reduced muscle tone (hypotonia) or rigidity
- Muscle contractions or spasticity
- Poor balance or ataxia

Fine Motor
- Reduced motor dexterity and tremors impairing cutting, drawing, or writing skills
- Problems with motor planning (dyspraxia) impairing dressing or assembly skills
- Problems with written output (dysgraphia) affecting written communication

5. Sensory Status Indicators

Hearing
- Partial or total hearing loss in one or both ears
- Difficulty understanding spoken language in a noisy environment
- Development of a "ringing sound" (tinnitus)

Vision
- Partial or total vision loss
- Visual field cuts (blind spots or areas)
- Impaired visual tracking (affecting reading, writing, driving, etc.)
- Visual blurring or double vision (diplopia)
- Unusual sensitivity to light

Other
- Unusual sensitivity to smells, tastes, tactile sensations

6. Health/Physical Status Indicators

- Physical limitations (restrictions from physical education, fatigue)
- Medical problems (seizures, motor spasticity, headaches, pain, dizziness, or vertigo)
- Medication needs (anticonvulsant, antidepressant, psychostimulant medications)
- Need for assistive devices (e.g., wheelchair, positioning tools, writing board, computer software)

7. Emotional and Social Development and Behavior Skills Indicators

- Agitated, depressed, anxious, or labile behaviors
- Immature, insensitive, or inappropriate behaviors
- Poor or unrealistic perceptions of self or abilities
- Low frustration tolerance and/or persistence

8. Functional Skills Indicators

- Problems in self-care (dressing, hygiene, feeding)
- Inability to work independently
- Inability to generalize information from one setting to another
- Problems orienting to time and place
- Difficulties with transitions or changes in routine

9. Vocational, Occupational Potential, and Secondary Transition Indicators

Jobs and Job Training
- Limited occupational interests
- Behavior/attitude interfering with employment
- Limited job-seeking or interview skills

Postsecondary Training
- Unrealistic goal setting
- Lack of awareness of postsecondary options
- Impaired self-advocacy skills and awareness of needs/accommodations

Community Participation
- Problems accessing reliable transportation
- Limited knowledge of legal rights
- Limited knowledge of and access to community services

Home Living
- Difficulties with medical management (self-administration of medication, making doctor appointments, etc.)
- Difficulties with money management, completing forms, understanding contractual agreements
- Difficulties with locating housing, maintaining a home (cleaning, repairs, etc.)

Recreation and Leisure
- Limited knowledge of and access to recreation/leisure options in community

Step III: Determine the Eligibility for a Diagnosis of a Traumatic Brain Injury

Important Point: The eligibility criteria for classifications under IDEA are not specifically stated under the law. Therefore, the eligibility criteria for a particular disability may differ from state to state. The information pertaining to "eligibility" is the authors' professional interpretation based on reviewing the states' guidelines and criteria for TBIs.

To identify as a student with a traumatic brain injury and therefore to be eligible for special education services, the IEP Committee documents that the following standards have been met:

- The IEP Committee must first ensure that a physician has completed medical documentation of the TBI and that the documentation is kept in the student's school file. The team must then verify that a functional impairment attributable to the TBI adversely affects the student's educational performance in one or more listed areas. This determination is made through a comprehensive special education evaluation.

- The team must have documentation by a physician or a health assessment statement that the student has an acquired injury to the brain caused by an external physical force. A key factor to consider when determining whether a student may be eligible for special education support under the category of TBI is the *type* of ABI. Medical documentation must be provided stating that the student's brain has been injured by an "external force." Students who have an acquired *nontraumatic* brain injury as a result of infection, cerebral vascular accidents, brain tumors, poisoning, or anoxic injury may have significant educational needs, but they do not meet TBI criteria. In such situations, eligibility under other special education categories could be considered by the educational team, depending on the presenting problems (Minnesota Department of Education, 2004).
- The team must have documentation by a physician or a health assessment statement of a medically verified TBI in the student's school file.
- The team should have some form of documentation by a physician or a health assessment statement that the student's condition is permanent or expected to last a certain length of time (e.g., more than 60 calendar days).
- The team must determine that a functional impairment attributable to the TBI adversely affects educational performance in one or more of the following areas:
    - Intellectual-cognitive
    - Academic
    - Communication
    - Motor
    - Sensory
    - Social-emotional-behavioral
    - Functional skills-adaptive behavior
- The team must determine that the functional impairments are *not* primarily the result of previously existing
    - Vision, hearing, or motor impairments
    - Emotional-behavioral disorders
    - Mental retardation
    - Language or specific learning disabilities
    - Environmental or economic disadvantage
    - Cultural differences
- The team must determine that the student needs special education services as a result of the disability.

Final Thoughts

A common misconception suggests that the degree of impairment generally correlates with the force of the impact. Although symptoms from a mild brain injury (e.g., postconcussive syndrome) might improve quickly, this may not always be the case. Diffuse damage to the brain can result from a mild brain injury, even when there is no loss of consciousness. In some situations, an injury that is considered "mild" may result in long-term cognitive and/or behavioral problems and the student may require special education services. Another misconception centers on the idea that young students' brains are more adaptable and pliant and therefore more resilient to the damaging effects of a brain injury (Minnesota Department of Education, 2004).

The difficulty experienced by students with TBI returning to school is that their educational and emotional needs are greatly different than what they were before the injury. Even though their disability has happened suddenly and traumatically, individuals with TBI can often remember how they were before the brain injury. This remembrance can therefore bring on many emotional and social changes and adverse reactions. In addition, the student's family, friends, and teachers also recall what the student was like before the injury. The differences in the student's behavior and medical condition usually lead all of them to experience difficulty changing or adjusting their expectations of the student (Hibbard, Gordon, Martin, Rashkin, & Brown, 2001).

Therefore, it is extremely important to plan carefully for the student's return to school. The school must play a very proactive role in assisting parents or guardians with the student's transition back to school. Planning for such a return should begin weeks before the student returns. As part of this process, the school will need to evaluate the student thoroughly so that both the school and parents or guardians will know what the student's educational needs are. The school and parents or guardians will then develop an IEP that addresses those educational needs (DePompei, Blosser, Savage, & Lash, 1998; National Dissemination Center for Children with Disabilities, 2004e).

14

Visual Impairment

Definition Under IDEA

Visual impairment including blindness means *an impairment in vision that, even with correction, adversely affects a student's educational performance. The term includes both partial sight and blindness.* (34 C.F.R. 300.7 (a)(c)(13))

Overview

The terms *partially sighted, low vision, legally blind*, and *totally blind* are used in the educational context to describe students with visual impairments. In terms of educational definitions, each is defined as follows:

Partially sighted indicates some type of visual problem has resulted in a need for special education (National Dissemination Center for Children with Disabilities, 2004f).

Low vision generally refers to a severe visual impairment, and one that is not necessarily limited to distance vision. It indicates that some functional vision exists, which can be used for gaining information through written means with or without the assistance of optical, nonoptical, or electronic devices (Kirk, Gallagher, & Anastasiow, 2000). Low vision applies to all individuals with sight who are unable to read the newspaper at a normal viewing distance, even with the aid of eyeglasses or contact lenses. They use a combination of vision and other senses to learn, although they may require adaptations in lighting or the size of print, and, sometimes, Braille.

Legal blindness is defined as visual acuity of 20/200 or less in the person's eye after correction, resulting in some confusion (National Dissemination Center for Children with Disabilities, 2004f).

Blindness implies that a student must learn and use Braille, a system of raised dots that the student reads tactilely), aural methods in order to receive instruction, or other nonvisual media (Heward, 2005; National Dissemination Center for Children with Disabilities, 2004f). It refers to a person with "no vision or only light perception" (the ability to determine the presence or absence of light; Huebner, 2000, p. 58).

Prevalence

The rate at which visual impairments occur in individuals under the age of 18 is 12.2 per 1,000. Severe visual impairments (legal or total blindness) occur at a rate of 0.06 per 1,000. The U.S. Department of Education (2004) reported that, during the 2003–2004 school year, 25,294 students ages 6 to 21 (or 0.4 percent of all students with disabilities) received special education services under the category of Visual Impairment. However, this number is not representative of the total number of students with visual impairments. This is because students with visual impairments will often have other disabilities as well, thereby being reported in another IDEA disability category (Mason, Davidson, & McNerney, 2000).

Determining the Presence of a Visual Impairment: Step by Step

Step I: Become Familiar With the Characteristics of Students With Visual Impairments

The effect of visual problems on a student's development depends on the severity, type of loss, age at which the condition appears, and overall functioning level of the student. Many students who have multiple disabilities may also have visual impairments resulting in motor, cognitive, and/or social DDs.

A young student with visual impairment has little reason to explore interesting objects in the environment and, thus, may miss opportunities to have experiences and to learn. This lack of exploration may continue until learning becomes motivating or until intervention begins.

Because the student cannot see parents or guardians or peers, he or she may be unable to imitate social behavior or understand non-verbal cues. Visual handicaps can create obstacles to a growing student's independence (National Dissemination Center for Children with Disabilities, 2004f).

Step II: Determine the Procedures and Assessment Measures

Evaluation for a visual impairment should include the following:

- Evaluation by a trained medical professional such as an ophthalmologist or optometrist, which documents the eye condition with the best possible correction
- A written functional vision and media assessment, completed or compiled by a licensed teacher of students with visual impairments, which includes
  - Observation of visual behaviors at school, home, or other environments
  - Educational implications of the eye condition based on information received from the eye report
  - Assessment and/or screening of expanded core curriculum skills (orientation and mobility, social interaction, visual efficiency, independent living, recreation and leisure, career education, assistive technology, and compensatory skills), as well as an evaluation of the student's reading and writing skills, needs, appropriate reading and writing media, and current and future needs for Braille
  - School history and levels of educational performance
  - Documentation and assessment of how visual impairment adversely affects educational performance in the classroom or learning environment

Besides these assessment measures, the following should be considered:

If a student is suspected of having a visual impairment under the definition set forth in IDEA, the following assessment measures should also be considered:

- An observation by a team member other than the student's general education teacher of the student's academic performance in a general classroom setting; or in the case of a student less than school age or out of school, an observation by a team member conducted in an age-appropriate environment

- A developmental history, if needed
- An assessment of intellectual ability
- Other assessments of the characteristics of speech and language impairments if the student exhibits impairments in any one or more of the following areas: cognition, fine motor, perceptual motor, communication, social or emotional, and perception or memory. These assessments are to be completed by specialists knowledgeable in the specific characteristics being assessed.
- A review of cumulative records, previous IEPs or IFSPs, and teacher-collected work samples
- If deemed necessary, a medical statement or health assessment statement indicating whether any physical factors may be affecting the student's educational performance
- Assessments to determine the impact of the suspected disability on the student's educational performance (ages kindergarten–21) or on the student's developmental progress (ages 3–kindergarten)
- Additional evaluations or assessments necessary to identify the student's educational needs

Step III: Determine the Eligibility for a Diagnosis of a Visual Impairment

Important Point: The eligibility criteria for classifications under IDEA are not specifically stated under the law. Therefore, the eligibility criteria for a particular disability may differ from state to state. The information pertaining to "eligibility" is the authors' professional interpretation based on reviewing the states' guidelines and criteria for visual impairments.

To make a final determination as to whether a student meets the criteria as a student with a visual impairment, the following steps should be taken:

- The team should review all existing information, including information from the parents or guardians, the student's cumulative records, and any previous IEPs or IFSPs. Evaluation documentation includes relevant information from these sources used in the eligibility determination.
- The team should review all of the assessments done by the multidisciplinary team to determine the impact of the disability.

- The team should then determine whether any additional assessments are necessary to identify the student's educational needs, including a functional assessment of the student's residual visual acuity or field of vision.
- Upon successful completion of the above, the team must then show that the student meets one of the following criteria:
  - The student's residual acuity is 20/70 or less in the better eye with correction.
  - The student's visual field is restricted to 20 degrees or less in the better eye.
  - The student has an eye pathology or a progressive eye disease that is expected to reduce either residual acuity or visual field to either an acuity level of 20/70 in the better eye or a visual field of 20 degrees or less in the better eye.
  - The assessment results of a licensed ophthalmologist or optometrist are inconclusive, or the student demonstrates inadequate use of residual vision.
- The team must also determine that the student's disability has an adverse impact on the student's educational performance (ages kindergarten–21) or on the student's developmental progress (ages 3–kindergarten).
- The team must also determine that the student needs special education services.
- The team must show that it has considered the student's special education eligibility and determined that the eligibility is not due to
  - A lack of appropriate instruction in reading, including the essential components of reading instruction (phonemic awareness, phonics, vocabulary development; reading fluency/oral reading skills; and reading comprehension strategies)
  - A lack of instruction in math or to limited English proficiency
- The team agrees that this student qualifies for special education.

Final Thoughts

In schools, students with visual impairments can often be easily identified if their visual loss is severe. However, many students have milder losses that are much more difficult to identify and may go several years without being recognized (Smith, Polloway, Patton, & Dowdy, 2004). Students with visual impairments can be grouped by their age of onset. Individuals who are born with visual impairments at birth or during infancy are considered to have congenital visual impairments, whereas those with visual impairments after the age of 2 are considered to have adventitious visual impairments (Huebner, 2000).

Most students with visual impairments are able to use vision for some activities. Families and professionals could encourage use of vision for activities where it is more efficient or can provide information. Use of vision in general activities can be determined by administration of a functional vision evaluation, an observational assessment completed by a certified teacher of visually impaired students. This assessment should include recommendations for adaptations, services, and instructional skills that will help the student learn to use vision appropriately (Erin, 2003).

Glossary

Ability grouping. The grouping of students based on their achievement in an area of study.

Accelerated learning. An educational process that allows students to progress through the curriculum at a faster pace.

Achievement. The level of a student's accomplishment on a test of knowledge or skill.

Adaptive behavior. The collection of conceptual, social, and practical skills that people have learned so they can function in their everyday lives.

Adaptive physical education. A modified program of instruction implemented to meet the needs of special students.

Advocate. An individual, either a parent or professional, who attempts to establish or improve services for exceptional students.

Age norms. Standards based on the average performance of individuals according to age groups.

Agnosia. A student's inability to recognize objects and their meaning, usually resulting from damage to the brain.

Amplification device. Any device that increases the volume of sound.

Anecdotal record. A procedure for recording and analyzing observations of a student's behavior; an objective, narrative description.

Annual goals. Yearly activities or achievements to be completed or attained by students with disabilities that are documented in individualized education programs (IEPs).

Aphasia. An acquired language disorder involving severe impairments in both comprehension and production.

Articulation. The production of distinct language sounds by the speech organs.

At risk. Having a high potential for experiencing future medical or learning problems.

Attention deficit/hyperactivity disorder (ADHD). A psychiatric condition characterized by poor attention, distractibility, impulsivity, and hyperactivity.

Baseline measure. The level or frequency of behavior prior to the implementation of an instructional procedure that will later be evaluated.

Behavior modification. The techniques used to change behavior by applying principles of reinforcement learning.

Bilingualism. The ability to speak two languages.

Career education. Instruction that focuses on the application of skills and content area information necessary to cope with the problems of daily life, independent living, and vocational areas of interest.

Categorical resource room. An auxiliary pull-out program that offers supportive services to exceptional students with the same disability.

Cognition. The mental process of knowing, including aspects such as awareness, perception, reasoning, and judgment.

Consultant teacher. A support specialist for students with disabilities who provides the services in the classroom.

Criterion-referenced tests. Tests in which the student is evaluated on his or her own performance according to a set of criteria and not in comparison to others.

Declassification. The process in which a student with a disability is no longer considered to be in need of special education services. This requires a meeting of the Eligibility Committee and can be requested by the parent or guardian, by the school, or by the student who has passed the age of 18.

Deficit. A level of performance that is less than expected for a student.

Desensitization. A technique used in reinforcement learning in which there is a weakening of a response, usually an emotional response.

Diagnosis. The specific disorder(s) identified as a result of some evaluation.

Distractibility. Difficulty in maintaining attention.

Due process. The legal steps and processes outlined in educational law that protect the rights of students with disabilities.

Dyscalculia. A serious learning disability in which the student has an inability to calculate, apply, solve, or identify mathematical functions.

Dysfluency. Difficulty in the production of fluent speech (e.g., stuttering).

Dysgraphia. A serious learning disability in which the student has an inability or loss of ability to write.

Dyslexia. A severe type of learning disability in which a student's ability to read is greatly impaired.

Dysorthographia. The learning disability associated with spelling.

Enrichment. Provision of a student with extra and more sophisticated learning experiences than those normally presented in the curriculum.

Etiology. The cause of a problem.

Exceptional student. Any child who requires special instruction or related services.

Free appropriate public education (FAPE). Special education and related services that are provided at public expense and conform to the state requirements and to the individual's IEP.

Group home. A residential living arrangement in which several adults with disabilities, especially those who are mentally retarded, reside with several supervisors without disabilities.

Habilitation. An educational approach used with exceptional students that is directed toward the development of the necessary skills required for successful adulthood.

Homebound instruction. A special education service in which teaching is provided by a specially trained instructor to students who are unable to attend school. A parent or guardian must always be present at the time of instruction. In some cases, the instruction may take place on a neutral site and not in the home or school.

Hyperactivity. Behavior that is characterized by excessive motor activity or restlessness.

Impulsivity. Non-goal-oriented activity exhibited by individuals who lack careful thought and reflection prior to a behavior.

Inclusion. Returning students with disabilities to their home school so that they may be educated in the same classroom with students who are not disabled.

Individualized education program (IEP). A written educational program that outlines the current levels of performance, related services, educational goals, and modifications for a student with a disability. This plan is developed by a team including the student's parent(s), teacher(s), and support staff.

Interdisciplinary team. The collective efforts of individuals from a variety of disciplines in assessing the needs of a student.

Intervention. Preventive, remedial, compensatory, or survival services made on behalf of an individual with a disability.

Itinerant teacher. A teacher hired by a school district to help in the education of a student with a disability. The teacher is employed by an outside agency and may be responsible for several students in several districts.

Learning disability. A disorder in one or more of the basic psychological processes involved in understanding or in using spoken or written language, which may manifest itself in an imperfect ability to listen, think, speak, read, write, spell, or do mathematical calculations.

Least restrictive environment (LRE). An educational setting for exceptional students and students with disabilities that minimizes their exclusion from students without disabilities.

Mainstreaming. The practice of educating exceptional students in the general classroom.

Mental age. The level of intellectual functioning based on the average for students of a given chronological age. When dealing with students with severe disabilities, the mental age may be more reflective of levels of ability than the chronological age.

Mental disability. A disability in which the individual's intellectual level is measured within the subaverage range and there are marked impairments in social competence.

Native language. The primary language used by an individual.

Noncategorical resource room. A resource room in a general education setting that provides services to students with several types of disabilities. The students with these disabilities are able to be maintained in a general school setting.

Norm-referenced tests. Tests that compare a student's performance to the performance of others on the same measure.

Occupational therapist. A professional who programs and/or delivers instructional activities and materials to help children and adults with disabilities participate in useful daily activities.

Paraprofessionals. A trained assistant who helps a classroom teacher provide instruction.

Physical therapist. A professional trained to assist individuals with disabilities and to help them maintain and develop muscular and orthopedic capability and make correct and useful movements.

PINS (person in need of supervision) petition. An appeal to a family court from the school or the parent to seek remedies for a student under the age of 16 who is out of control in attendance, behavior, or some socially inappropriate or destructive pattern.

Positive reinforcement. Any stimulus or event that occurs after a behavior has been exhibited that increases the possibility of that behavior occurring in the future.

Pupil personnel team. A group of professionals from the same school who meet at regular intervals to discuss students' problems and offer suggestions or directions for resolution.

Pupils with special educational needs (PSEN). Students defined as having mathematics and reading achievement lower than the 23rd percentile and requiring remediation. These students are not considered to have disabilities but are entitled to assistance to elevate their academic levels.

Related services. Services provided to students with disabilities to enhance their ability to learn and function in the least restrictive environment. Such services may include in-school counseling and speech and language services.

Remediation. An educational program designed to teach students to overcome some deficit or disability through education and training.

Resource room. An auxiliary service provided to students with disabilities for part of the school day. It is intended to service students' special needs so that they can be maintained within the least restrictive educational setting.

Response to intervention (RTI). A three-tiered model established under IDEA 2004 as an alternative to the discrepancy model for determining whether a student has a learning disability.

Screening. The process of examining groups of students to identify at-risk students.

Section 504. Part of the Rehabilitation Act of 1973 in which guarantees are provided for the civil rights of children and adults with disabilities. It also applies to the provision of services for students whose disabilities are not severe enough to warrant classification but could benefit from supportive services and classroom modifications.

Self-contained class. A special classroom for exceptional students, usually located within a general school building.

Sheltered workshops. A transitional or long-term work environment for individuals with disabilities who cannot, or who are preparing for, work in a regular setting. Within this setting the individual can learn to perform meaningful, productive tasks and receive payment.

Student study team (SST). School-based, problem-solving groups whose mission is to assist teachers, administrators, and school staff with intervention strategies for dealing with the academic and social-emotional behavioral needs of general education students. Such groups seek creative ways to maximize the use of available resources and formalize what is already being done for students in the building.

Surrogate parent. A person other than the student's natural parent who has legal responsibility for the student's care and welfare.

Token economy. A system of reinforcing various behaviors through the delivery of tokens. These tokens can take the form of stars, points, candy, chips, and so on.

Total communication. The approach to the education of students who are deaf that combines oral speech, sign language, and finger spelling.

Underachievement. A discrepancy between a student's actual academic achievement and expected academic achievement. It is important that the school identify the underlying causes of such underachievement because it may be a symptom of a more serious problem.

Vocational rehabilitation. A program designed to help adults with disabilities obtain and hold jobs.

References and Suggested Readings

American Speech-Language-Hearing Association. (2005). *Speech-language disorders and the speech-language pathologist*. Retrieved September 10, 2005, from http://www.asha.org/students/professions/overview/sld.htm

Avramidis, E., & Bayliss, P. (2000). A survey into mainstream teachers' attitudes towards the inclusion of children with special educational needs in the ordinary school in one local education authority. *Educational Psychology: Dorchester on Thames, 20*(2), 191.

Berliner, D. (2006). Our impoverished view of educational reform. *Teachers College Record, 108*(6), 949–995.

Best, S. J., Heller, K. W., & Bigge, J. L. (2005). *Teaching individuals with physical or multiple disabilities* (5th ed.). Upper Saddle River, NJ: Merrill/Prentice Hall.

Bowe, F. (2005). *Making inclusion work*. Upper Saddle River, NJ: Merrill/Pearson.

Boyer, L., & Lee, C. (2001). Converting challenge to success: Supporting a new teacher of students with autism. *Journal of Special Education, 35*(2), 75–83. Retrieved February 26, 2002, from Eric/Ebsco database.

Brain Injury Association of America. (2004). *Causes of brain injury*. McLean, VA: Author. Retrieved March 13, 2005, from http://www.biausa.org/Pages/causes_of_braininjury.html

Bureau of Labor Statistics, U.S. Department of Labor. (2005). *Occupational outlook handbook, 2004–05 edition, teachers—Special education*. Retrieved November 28, 2005, from http://www.bls.gov/oco/ocos070.htm

Calderon, R., & Naidu, S. (2000). Further support for the benefits of early identification and intervention for children with hearing loss. *Volta Review, 100*(5), 53–84.

California Deaf-Blind Services. (1996). *Deaf-blindness*. Retrieved August 10, 2005, from http://www.sfsu.edu/~cadbs/Eng016.html

Case, R. (2005). Language difference or learning disability? *The Clearing House, 78*(3), 127.

Chandler, J. (2004). *What is a learning disorder?* Retrieved September 10, 2005, from http://www.klis.com/chandler/

Clark, E., Russman, S., & Orme, S. (1999). Traumatic brain injury: Effects on school functioning and intervention strategies [Electronic version]. *School Psychology Review, 28,* 242–50.

Closs, A. (2000). *The education of children with medical conditions.* London: David Fulton Publishers.

Coffey, K., & Obringer, S. (2004). A case study on autism. *Education: Chula Vista, 124*(4), 632.

Colarusso, R., & O'Rourke, C. (2004). *Special education for all teachers.* Dubuque, IA: Kendall/Hunt.

Cullen, J. B., and Rivkin, S. G. (2003). The role of special education in school choice. In C. Hoxby (Ed.), *The economics of school choice* (pp. 67–106). Chicago: University of Chicago Press.

Deaf Blind Services Division, Utah Schools for the Deaf and the Blind. (n.d.). *Deaf-blindness.* Retrieved April 2, 2006, from http://www.dblink.org/lib/dish/general_learning_char.pdf

Department for Learning and Educational Achievement. (2006). *Student study teams: Mission statement.* Golden, CO: Jeffco Public Schools.

DePompei, R., Blosser, J., Savage, R., & Lash, M. (1998). *Special education: IEP checklist for a student with a brain injury.* Wolfeboro, NH: L&A Publishing/Training.

Deutsch-Smith, D. (2004). *Introduction to special education: Teaching in an age of opportunity* (5th ed.). Boston: Allyn & Bacon.

Eigenbrood, R. (2005). A survey comparing special education services for students with disabilities in rural faith based and public school settings. *Remedial and Special Education, 26*(1), 16.

Erin, J. N. (2003). *Educating students with visual impairments.* Arlington, VA: The Council for Exceptional Children.

Friend, M. (2005). *Special education: Contemporary perspectives for school professionals.* Boston: Allyn & Bacon.

Friend, M., & Bursuck, W. D. (2002). *Including students with special needs: A practical guide for classroom teachers* (3rd ed.). Boston: Allyn & Bacon.

Fuchs, L. S., & Fuchs, D. (2001). Principles for sustaining research-based practice in the schools: A case study. *Focus on Exceptional Children, 33*(6), 1–14.

Fuchs, L. S., Fuchs, D., & Speece, D. L. (2002). Treatment validity as a unifying construct for identifying learning disabilities. *Learning Disability Quarterly, 25,* 33–45.

Galley, M. (2003). Oklahoma: Special education bears brunt of state aid cuts. *Education Week, 23*(1), 26.

Gargiulo, R. M. (2004). *Special education in contemporary society: An introduction to exceptionality.* Belmont, CA: Thompson-Wadsworth.

Giler, J. Z. (2000). *Socially ADDept™: A manual for parents of children with ADHD and/or learning disabilities.* CES Continuing Education Seminars. Retrieved September 13, 2005, from http://www.ldonline.org/article.php?max=20&id=770&loc=47

Grandin, T. (2001, June). *Teaching tips for children and adults with autism.* Retrieved February 19, 2002, from http://www.autism.org/temple/tips.html

Groves, M. (2001, June 14). The nation: Routine autism screening should be done at an early age. *Los Angeles Times,* pp. A1, A4. Retrieved March 12, 2002, from Academic Universe/Lexis-Nexis database.

Hallahan, D. P., & Kauffman, J. M. (2006). *Exceptional learners: Introduction to special education* (10th ed.). Needham Heights, MA: Allyn & Bacon.

Hardman, M. L., Drew, C. J., & Egan, M. W. (2005). *Human exceptionality: School, community, and family.* Boston: Allyn & Bacon.

Heller, K. W., Dangel, H., & Sweatman, L. (1995). Systematic selection of adaptations for students with muscular dystrophy. *Journal of Developmental and Physical Disabilities, 7,* 253–265.

Heller, K. W., Frederic, L. D., Best, S., Dykes, M. K., & Cohen, E. T. (2000). Specialized health care procedures in the schools: Training and service delivery. *Exceptional Children, 66,* 173–186.

Heward, W. L. (2006). *Exceptional children: An introduction to special education* (8th ed.). Upper Saddle River, NJ: Pearson Education.

Hibbard, M., Gordon, W., Martin, T., Rashkin, B., & Brown, M. (2001). *Students with traumatic brain injury: Identification, assessment, and classroom accommodations.* New York: Research and Training Center on Community Integration of Individuals with Traumatic Brain Injury.

Holden-Pitt, L., & Diaz, J. (1998). Thirty years of the Annual Survey of Deaf and Hard-of-Hearing Children and Youth: A glance over the decades. *American Annals of the Deaf, 142*(2), 72–76.

Huebner, K. M. (2000). Visual impairment. In M. C. Holbrook & A. J. Koenig (Eds.), *Foundations of education: History and theory of teaching children and youths with visual impairments* (2nd ed., pp. 55–76). New York: American Foundation for the Blind Press.

Hunt, N., & Marshall, K. (2005). *Exceptional children and youth* (4th ed.). Boston: Houghton Mifflin.

Individuals with Disabilities Education Improvement Act (IDEA) of 2004, PL 108-446, 20 U.S.C. §§ 1400 et seq.

Iowa Department of Education. (1997). *Assessment and decision making for special education entitlement: Technical assistance guide for mental disability.* Des Moines: Bureau of Special Education, Iowa Department of Education.

Jensen, M. (2005). *Introduction to emotional and behavioral disorders: Recognizing and managing problems in the classroom.* Upper Saddle River, NJ: Merrill/Prentice Hall.

Keyser-Marcus, L., Briel, L., Sherron-Targett, P., Yasuda, S., Lohnson, S., & Wehman, P. (2002). Enhancing the schooling of students with traumatic brain injury. *Teaching Exceptional Children, 34*(4), 62–67.

Kirk, S., Gallagher, J., & Anastasiow, N. (2000). *Educating exceptional children* (9th ed.). Boston: Houghton Mifflin.

Knich, D. (2005, October 31). Inclusion helps students feel part of mainstream. *The Island Packet.* Retrieved January 30, 2007, from http:// www .islandpacket.com

LDOnline. (2005). *Learning disabilities.* Retrieved September 10, 2005, from http://www.LDOnline.org

Leibrock, C., & Terry, J. E. (1999). *Beautiful universal design.* Hoboken, NJ: John Wiley.

Lerner, J. W. (2003). *Learning disabilities: Theories, diagnosis, and teaching strategies* (9th ed.). Boston: Houghton Mifflin.

Luckasson, R. (2002). *Mental retardation: Definition, classification, and systems of supports* (10th ed.). Washington, DC: American Association on Mental Retardation.

Marcus, L. (2002, January 10). *Inclusion for children with autism: The TEACCH position.* Retrieved February 19, 2002, from http://www.teacch.com/inclus.htm

Mason, C., Davidson, R., & McNerney, C. (2000). *National plan for training personnel to serve children with blindness and low vision.* Reston, VA: Council for Exceptional Children.

Mesibov, G. (2002, January 10). *Learning styles of students with autism.* Retrieved February 19, 2002, from http://www.teacch.com/ed

Mestel, R. (2001, March 12). Special report: Autism. *Los Angeles Times,* p. S1. Retrieved March 12, 2002, from Academic Universe/Lexis-Nexis database.

Michaud, L. J., Semel-Concepcion, J., Duhaime, A. C., & Lazar, M. F. (2002). Traumatic brain injury. In M. L. Batshaw (Ed.), *Children with disabilities* (5th ed., pp. 525–548). Baltimore: Paul H. Brookes.

Minnesota Department of Education. (2004). *Special education evaluation and services for students with traumatic brain injury: A manual for Minnesota educators.* Retrieved November 1, 2006, from http://www.education.state.mn.us/mde/static/001755.pdf

National Dissemination Center for Children with Disabilities. (2004a). *Deafness and hearing loss.* Retrieved February 5, 2007, from http://www.nichcy.org/pubs/factshe/fs3txt.htm

National Dissemination Center for Children with Disabilities. (2004b). *Learning disabilities: A fact sheet.* Retrieved September 10, 2006, from http://www.nichcy.org/pubs/factshe/fs7txt.htm

National Dissemination Center for Children with Disabilities. (2004c). *Mental retardation.* Retrieved July 13, 2005, from http://www.nichcy.org/pubs/factshe/fs8txt.htm

National Dissemination Center for Children with Disabilities. (2004d). *Severe and/or multiple disabilities: Fact sheet #10.* Retrieved April 5, 2006, from http://www.nichcy.org/pubs/factshe/fs10txt.htm

National Dissemination Center for Children with Disabilities. (2004e). *Traumatic brain injury: Fact sheet #18.* Retrieved April 4, 2006, from http://www.nichcy.org/pubs/factshe/fs18txt.htm

National Dissemination Center for Children with Disabilities (2004f). *Visual impairments.* Retrieved February 5, 2007, from http://www.nichcy.org/pubs/factshe/fs13txt.htm

National Joint Committee on Learning Disabilities. (2005). *Responsiveness to intervention and learning disabilities.* Washington, DC: Author. Retrieved January 30, 2007, from http://www.ldonline.org/about/partners/njcld

National Library of Congress. (2005). *Mental retardation.* Retrieved October 20, 2006, from http://www.nlm.nih.gov/medlineplus/ency/article/001523.htm

NEC Foundation of America. (2001). *Multiple disabilities: Educational implications.* Retrieved February 4, 2006, from http://www.teachersandfamilies.com/sped/prof/multdis/education.html

Ohio Coalition for the Education of Children with Disabilities. (2005). *What are multiple disabilities?* Retrieved March 18, 2006, from http://www .ocecd.org/ocecd/h_docs/whataremult.cfm

Olson, J. L., & Platt, J. M. (2000). *Teaching children and adolescents with special needs.* Upper Saddle River, NJ: Prentice Hall.

Palmer, A. (2002, January 10). *Strategies for surviving middle school with an included child with autism.* Retrieved February 19, 2002, from http:// www.teacch.com/survmidd.htm

Pierangelo, R., & Giuliani, G. (2006a). *Assessment in special education: A practical approach* (2nd ed.). Boston: Allyn & Bacon.

Pierangelo, R., & Giuliani, G. (2006b). *Learning disabilities: A practical approach to foundations, assessment, diagnosis and teaching.* Boston: Allyn & Bacon.

Pierangelo, R., & Giuliani, G. (in press). *Educator's diagnostic manual of disabilities and disorders.* San Francisco: Jossey-Bass/John Wiley.

Ramey, C. T., & Ramey, S. L. (1999). *Right from birth.* New York: Goddard Press.

Sirvis, B. (1988). Physical disabilities. In E. Meyen & T. Skrtic (Eds.), *Exceptional children and youth: An introduction* (3rd ed.). Denver, CO: Love Publishing.

Smith, T. E. C., Polloway, E. A., Patton, J. R., & Dowdy, C. A. (2004). *Teaching students with special needs in inclusive settings* (4th ed.). Needham Heights, MA: Allyn & Bacon.

Stowitschek, J., & Lovit, T. (2001). Patterns of collaboration in secondary education for youth with special needs: Profiles of three high schools. *Urban Education, 36*(1), 93.

Temple, L. (2000, February 15). Disputed health duties injected into teaching of disabled. *USA Today,* p. 9D.

Texas School for the Blind and Visually Impaired. (2003). *Multiple disabilities.* Retrieved March 2, 2006, from http://www.tsbvi.edu/Education/ infant/page5.htm

Thurlow, M. (2005). State policies on assessment participation and accommodations of students with disabilities. *The Journal of Special Education, 28*(4), 232.

Turnbull, A., Turnbull, R., & Wehmeyer, M. L. (2006). *Exceptional lives: Special education in today's schools* (5th ed.). Upper Saddle River, NJ: Pearson.

Turnbull, R., Turnbull, A., Shank, M., & Smith, S. J. (2004). *Exceptional lives: Special education in today's schools* (4th ed.). Englewood Cliffs, NJ: Prentice Hall.

U.S. Department of Education. (2000). *Twenty-second annual report to Congress on the implementation of IDEA.* Washington, DC: Author.

U.S. Department of Education. (2001). *Twenty-third annual report to Congress on the implementation of IDEA.* Washington, DC: Author.

U.S. Department of Education. (2004). *Twenty-sixth annual report to Congress on the implementation of IDEA.* Washington, DC: Author.

Winerip, M. (2005, October 19). Keeping special ed on the radar. *New York Times.*

Wisniewski, R. (2001). *US president signs education bill: What does this mean for autism?* Retrieved February 19, 2002, from http://www.autism-society .org/news/2001education_bill.html

Young, S. (2005). *No Child Left Behind: History.* Retrieved September 3, 2006, from www.ncsi.org/programs/educ/NCLBhistory.htm

Index

CORWIN PRESS

The Corwin Press logo—a raven striding across an open book—represents the union of courage and learning. Corwin Press is committed to improving education for all learners by publishing books and other professional development resources for those serving the field of PreK–12 education. By providing practical, hands-on materials, Corwin Press continues to carry out the promise of its motto: **"Helping Educators Do Their Work Better."**

Made in the USA
Las Vegas, NV
12 January 2021